UNDERSTANDING DESTINY

Ayesha Dempsey

SERPENT BOOKS - LONDON, UK

A Serpent New Age Book

Published by Serpent Books
Copyright 2002, Ayesha Dempsey

All rights reserved under International and Pan-American
Copyright Conventions.
Published in the USA by Serpent Books.
Printed by Gooch

ISBN 1-930024-00-2

Manufactured in the United Kingdom

First Edition June 2002

CHAPTER 1
INTRODUCTION

In this galaxy, there is only one great Spirit who prepares a planet for creation at any given time. This entity originally was the God of the house of Leo. His reign ended when he was overrun at Heliopolis, and burnt at the stake by the Matriarch's soldiers approximately one thousand four hundred years ago, and I shall refer to him as 'the Creator.' He began preparing the planet for habitation some three hundred thousand years ago, and that creation is spoken about in Genesis 1.

Immediately following creation, an Incarnating fraternity moves into a planet's sphere to work towards one or the other predetermined outcome. The whole of the universe is about evolving

1

the spirit in consciousness.

Following the creation spoken about in Genesis 1, the Matriarch entered the earth plane. They originally arrived with a band of slave-soldiers they tattooed from head to toe to mark them as property. As they claimed they wished to evolve the slaves to a higher level of consciousness on a planet with water, the Creator allowed them entry, provided they left within one age. Their leaving however, never came about. They have been around ever since, and have tried to enrich the gene quality of their spirit collective by usurping spirits left outside by other spirit houses. To this end, they endeavoured to make Matriarchal rules part of the 'law' that determined whether or not spirits were collected by other collectives.

The Matriarch began creating without permission in North America first, then in South America, and then in Africa. They created mainly useless reptiles, and humans who could not replenish the earth, and almost destroyed the planet's resources.

The most recent age of Taurus however, brought the Matriarch the participation he sought, when the Patriarch delivered the female collective unto the Matriarch following the human female choosing sexual freedom at the start of the most recent age of Taurus, see 'The Snake, the Woman, and the Tree,' below. This state of affairs ended at the turn of the last century when a new Incarnating fraternity brought female empowerment, in spite of attempts at perpetuating Matriarchal, and Patriarchal male-female value transfers in the West.

The creation spoken about in Genesis 1 spanned seven great ages. It started at the beginning of the great age of Aquarius about three hundred and eleven thousand years ago, and ended in the great age of Leo about one hundred and fifty thousand years ago.

Creation on a planet always begins during a great age of Aquarius, and at the beginning of an age of Aquarius. The reason is that Aquarius is a wild card that does not take sides, yet is committed to the direction chosen. In the case of creation for example, Aquarius is uncompromising in its commitment that there will be life, but cannot be involved in favouring the survival of one life form over another. That is for each life form to decide.

On 25 February 2001, a new age of Aquarius began simultaneously with another great age of Aquarius. All in all, evolution on planet earth has spanned twelve great ages, or one great year, and that is the total time given an Incarnating fraternity to finish what they began. After this, the planet is usually destroyed, or given a new Incarnating force.

Around twenty seven thousand years ago, on the cusp of a new great age of Pisces, and at the start of a new age of Aquarius, the Creator returned to earth with the Patriarch, following a cataclysmic destruction of the planet, initiated by the Creator to rid himself of Matriarchal participation. The Patriarch was the head of a group of twenty thousand people, and their arrival was followed by the arrival of a group of two hundred thousand so-called 'giants,' spoken about in Genesis 6.

The Matriarchs were given to human sacrifice, and karmic enslavement of husbands, and children, two concepts I deal with, below. In addition, they had created a Satan-prototype called Apep, figure 1. This spirit entity presided over the seances they held to commemorate their Judaic principles, (Judaic here being derived from the word 'Judas.') They thus celebrated their tendency to undermine those who trusted them, and who relied on them for safety.

3

The Matriarchs had created mainly useless reptilian animals from their own genes, and the earth's resources were being squandered supporting life that consumed resources, without giving in return. As the Creator approached, he recalled the spirit of the earth, which gathered itself together over the North pole, where the rain that fell turned to ice.

The atmosphere having gone, refraction thereby lost, the sun's light was immediately 'darkened,' figure 2. The men created during the great age of Gemini, and at the beginning of the age of Aquarius, spoken about in Genesis 1 (by this time corrupted by Matriarchal values), took refuge as best they could. Everything became dormant, and the Matriarchs receded into a bunker system the Matriarch had built in various parts of the world, where oxygen, and heat were relatively more available than on the surface. They took in all their slaves, and immediately converted some into dried meat. The remaining slaves lived on corn they produced underground [in the absence of sunlight, but in the presence of water,] and artificial light. They were made to cook over fires made from human excrement to ensure physical weakness in the men whose uprising the Matriarch feared. [Sacrificing the strong to ensure the survival of the weak is a Matriarchal value.]

As the nutritional value of the food down-scaled over time, the Matriarchs dried the meat of each slave who died underground. In response to the frigidity of the atmosphere, their bodies hardened, halved in size, their eye colour changed from blue to brown, and they became hermaphroditic.

By the time the atmosphere was reinstated one hundred and twenty years after it was lifted, the Matriarchs emerged, carefully concealing their presence. All were tiny, had dark eyes, red skins, and dark hair, and they numbered twenty. The restructuring that followed the return of the Creator during the previous age of Aquarius, is spoken about in Genesis 2.

He arrived with twenty thousand Patriarchs, and two hundred thousand giants. The giants settled here, but had little interest in engineering new life forms. They were mainly interested in astrology, and building stone structures. Little is known about them, save that their women had blonde hair and blue eyes. The women were very beautiful, pursued studious activities, and researched herbal medicine. The Matriarchal order soon sought to learn about herbal medicine, and proceeded to incorporate it into their 'magic.' The Patriarchs on the other hand, set about trying to uplift the consciousness of their collective by trying to attach themselves to the giants' women through marriage (a karmic concept I deal with, below.)

Contrary to popular belief, earth is not one of many planets that support life, but indeed one of about two hundred thousand planets that support life.

The problem of creation is that suns do not come ready with planets orbiting them. This condition need be brought about. Some suns have sister suns. (Yellow dwarf suns are favoured, as the white dwarfs are toxic, the blue giants are completely beyond approach, and the red dwarfs are too cold). The Creator picks one sun to sacrifice to creation.

At the time that creation begins, he induces atomic fission on the surface of the sun he decides to sacrifice. This process is referred to as 'induction,' and it triggers an explosion of the sun. Induction always is effected at the beginning of a great age of Pisces, the age of division of partnerships. The whole of the universe is about astronomical symbolism. Astronomy, and its sister science, astrology were abused by the Matriarchs who sacrificed children born under astrological conditions deemed to indicate that a child incarnated from the house of the Patriarch. As a result, astrology fell into disfavour, as it became associated with the promotion of infant sacrifice, cannibalism, and the practice of arranged marriage, all associated with Matriarchy, which in turn, became associated with witch craft.

Obviously, a sun can be destroyed without outcome, and this happens about as often as not. If the fragmentation is too severe, as almost happened in this solar system, the planets are too small to be viable. A planet is not viable when the core is small and not liquid. Simplistically stated, fission induces both explosion, and solidifying at the outer extremes as energy is converted to matter.

As the sun rips apart, the major fragments fall into orbit on the same orbital plane that the sacrificed sun occupied.

Water, and atmosphere on a planet do not come with the territory, but is manufactured and integrated, shortly after a spirit is brought in from the solar system occupied by the Creative force of the time. This spirit envelopes a planet, and its energy constitutes what is known as 'atmosphere.' This spirit energy energises life, retains atmosphere and water, and enables refraction of the sun's light, figure 3.

The ideal core is relatively large, liquid, and contains an element of hydrogen, without which creation is not possible. This facilitates the creation of water, while obviating the necessity to take large quantities of hydrogen to a planet. The Creator creates water in great quantities by infusing hydrogen with oxygen, and simultaneously, hydrogen with oxygen in the presence of nitrogen [in a plus minus ten to one ratio, that ensures stability,] to create atmosphere.

The presence of sulphur enables the first life supporting foundations to be laid. Simplistically stated, sulphur is the substance that enables creation, although it has to be said that sulphur is infused with energy on the back of carbon, to bring about DNA. The point is that, carbon in the absence of sulphur is of no use to any Creator.

In addition to the risk of the fragments being too small to sustain life, the sun that is sacrificed sometimes loses all her liquid fuel at the moment of induction. For this reason, the chunks that come into existence have to be large enough that the gravitation within the centre is able to pull the chunk together without the liquid spilling out. This is a massive challenge, and it often goes wrong. At the very centre, where the sacrificed sun's core was at the moment of induction, a planet like Jupiter comes into existence. It is of no use to anyone, and it tries to revert back to what it was before induction.

The existence of other planets in the same solar system as the planet on which creation takes place, is deemed essential by those who create. No life can exist on a planet without a moon, as those who create seek to incarnate those who are in their likeness in circumstances of astronomical symbolism, the moon symbolising the female principle. The whole of the universe, the whole of the spirit, is about symbolism.

Following induction, the new solar system is left to pan out for a period of one great age.

In any solar system, only one, or two orbits are able to sustain life. In this solar system, only the third orbit is able to sustain life, due to the orbits being far apart. Should a sun be extremely viable, as earth's sun indeed is, a planet is sometimes bumped out of its orbit towards the end of its life, and replaced with a planet already partly evolved, like Venus for example. [It has been postulated that, during the age of Aries, and without the Patriarch's permission, Lucifer brought Venus into the planetary system. Whether he arrived on Venus, or on a meteorite is not certain. What is known as that there was a measure of upheaval, and a proliferation of insects, especially flies and locusts, as a direct result of a foreign body entering the planetary system. [Interestingly, the Alter Ego is associated with disease, and disease is symbolised by the house fly, while the Matriarch was symbolised by the locust during the age of Aries. Significantly perhaps, Apep was immediately replaced in the Matriarchal order by Lucifer, due to Apep's having refused to overlay human women with masculine energy to render them more sexually attractive to other women.]

The third stage of planetary preparation immediately follows the creation of atmosphere, and water. Within the same twenty four hour day [and its inception is always astronomically determined,] the first volcanic eruption on earth was induced by atomic fusion, and the first continent was born. In earth's case, Mars, Jupiter, and Saturn [the masculine planets,] aligned with Earth. From the moment the first eruption is induced, a planet has a limited lifespan. As pressure is lost, the core gradually solidifies. The moment that more than 30% of a planet's core solidifies, resources begin dwindling. At 50%, the planet becomes inactive, and life becomes extinct.

The planet is set turning on its own axis at the moment of induction. A planet that exits motionless, cannot be used for creation, as often happens. Sometimes meteorites are used to induce rotation, but it is usually not successful. As the length of day on a life sustaining planet is extremely important, the speed at which the planet turns on its axis is important. To effect optimum rotation of as many planets as possible, induction is controlled as closely as possible.

Plant life need be well established before animal life begins, as animals spontaneously begin preying on plants. All life begins with the one-celled plant. As it is illegal to take plants, or animals from one planet to another, plant life need be started from scratch.

The one-celled plant is extremely difficult to bring into existence from energy combining with one molecule of matter in such a way that the molecule absorbs the energy on which DNA is digitally inscribed. [Life giving energy has DNA digitally inscribed on it, as a body cell has DNA physically inscribed on it.] Simplistically stated, the molecule of matter absorbs the energy plus the genes inscribed on the energy as a cell nucleus. [Carbon simply absorbs energy.] The will to proliferate itself, is obviously one thing inscribed on the genetic material. After about a month of struggle in the laboratory, cell division spontaneously occurs for the first time. After the hundredth molecule spontaneously begins dividing in the laboratory, the first attempt is made at placing the molecules in their envisaged 'natural' environment.

To effect this outcome, one molecule of matter receives as much energy as is contained within the energy field of a human. This is the amount of energy invested during the very first stages of creation. Once this stage of creation is well established, energy investment in subsequent life forms is less expensive as the genes absorbed into the original molecules can be altered to form variant life forms without more energy being invested [energy by this time in fact being produced.] From here, complex life forms can be created within about one hundred thousand years.

At the beginning of creation, no intervention is attempted at determining which molecule lives off which one. That arrangement is arbitrary, and comes into existence as a result of a psychic contract between one-celled animals. [Cannibalism characterises the most primitive life forms, before those that are stronger have eaten all that are weaker. At this point, cannibalism ends, and genetic diversion spontaneously ensues, as remaining cannibals determine who will be sacrificed to whom. The diversion that follows results in the formation of two energy collectives: one proliferating hunters, the other proliferating the hunted.]

The hunted, however, still need eat, and usually take to drawing sustenance from their environment. With time, they evolve characteristics that enhance their ability to draw moisture and food from the environment in which they find themselves at the time. Their individual appearance changes as the collective 'character' they acquire to survive and function in their specified environments, gradually emerges. There is no intervention here at all, save that the spirit collective to which each belongs gradually splits into ever more specific sub-collectives that each incarnates increasingly specialised life forms.

Contrary to popular belief, all life does not evolve spontaneously from here. The eventual intended climax of creation is always kept in mind, and genetic engineering guides evolution along.

A collective loses the will to live when too many adjustments need be made to continue existing in a way that makes its existence worth its while. A collective's life is worth its while, when it is able to do its will. In the face of less evolved species proliferating among them, and directing inhibiting signals in their direction, a collective experiences its existence as little more than a struggle.

Once this level of sophistication is reached, consciousness is in danger of reverting again to a stage of greater entropy, as the species that once existed for love of itself increasingly withdraws from the life situation. At this point, the more evolved collective is in danger of being invaded by the rival collective as rival species' collectives begin encroaching on the territory occupied by the evolved collective.

Psychological, rather than environmental factors invariably precede extinction, and those factors relate to stress, brought about by one species being under constant pressure to give energy to a less evolved collective. The rival species act in unison, as if an agenda against the evolved species is known to each individual organism of the rival species. The evolved species gradually becomes caught in a conflict between generating energy to give away, and committing suicide to rid itself of the demands for energy posed by the rival species. This applies to all species, from the simplest one celled varieties to the most complex mammals.

At the beginning of the most recent age of Taurus, the man created at the beginning of the age of Aquarius, twenty thousand years earlier, was ousted from the garden of Eden. [Figure 4 shows the bovine being imbued with the will to sacrifice itself to man's survival needs at the beginning of the most recent age of Taurus.]

THE SIGNIFICANCE OF AGES

Astronomical cycles of precession are firstly divided into great years that span time periods of three hundred and eleven thousand and forty years. Secondly, they are divided into great ages that last twenty five thousand nine hundred and twenty years each, and thirdly, into ages of two thousand one hundred and sixty years each. Each great year thus consists of twelve great ages, and each great age in turn, consists of twelve ages. Each age carries the name of an astronomical sign, as does each great age.

Not only did a new age of Aquarius begin at the start of 2001, a new great age of Aquarius began around the same time. At the beginning of each new age the Incarnating spirit begins a new cycle of growth in consciousness. At this time, a new blueprint is given man, whose purpose is to bring the human experience in line with the symbolic meaning of the new age. This immediately results in the emergence of a new kind of human consciousness. All spirits deemed unable to adapt are discarded. This, in turn, prevents the human experience from stagnating.

The beginning of a great age has special significance in the eyes of the universe. Not only does it mark the beginning of a new period of growth, it marks the beginning of a new kind of life experience, which presupposes the emergence of a new kind of man.

Great ages are divided into ages of Patriarchy, Matriarchy, Benign Intervention, and Division, and each Incarnating spirit group in the universe represents one of either Division, Benign Intervention, Patriarchy, or Matriarchy. The paradigm for the age of Aquarius, is Division.

THE AGE OF AQUARIUS

The age of Aquarius represents the beginning of the 'fulfil

ment of the law.' The fulfilment of the law however, does not refer
to the ending of Moses' law, as the church has suggested. The fulfilment of the law refers to the ending of the law given Adam in
Eden, and the beginning of man's awareness of himself as a spirit
entity, aware that physical life exists to support the spirit's evolution. The paradigm of Aquarius represents knowledge about
how life relates to the spirit's evolution, enabling each person to
serve the purpose of the higher god: the spirit of self, and that
has never been understood to be the reason for man's existence.
Knowing how the human psyche hangs together enables each person in his or her own way, to maximize outcomes.

Before continuing it is necessary the reader familiarise himself, or herself with each of the paradigms of Matriarchy, Patriarchy,
Benign Intervention, and Division, the latter introduced into the
earth experience for the first time, one hundred years ago.

MATRIARCHY

A Matriarch is not a motherly woman. A Matriarch is either a
man, or a woman, incarnated from the spirit collective of the
Matriarch. The Matriarch represents the embodiment of 'evil,' evil
being the will to sacrifice, or disempower that which will not be weak.

The Matriarchal collective consists of a group of hermaphroditic spirits, fundamentally opposed to individuality, who mainly
incarnate as women. The original Matriarchal archetype is symbolised by Beb, figure 5, and the 'dog spirit,' or 'the keeper of contracts,' figure 6. [Bringing karmic contracts into existence is the
major thrust of Matriarchy.]

The Matriarch first began incarnating on earth about one

13

hundred and fifty thousand years ago, after the Creator left the planet to create elsewhere.

Using genetic engineering, the Matriarchs created a variety of mainly useless reptilian creatures that were not part of the food chain. They first consumed the earth's resources before proceeding to consume one another, and then to consume people. At this time, the Matriarch began selectively sacrificing people to man-eating reptiles. In the end, these creatures came in for feeding at sunrise, at which time humans who had already been killed on a pyre were fed to them. Those who only took live bait were placed in captivity, and kept for entertainment purposes. This was the beginning of gladiator sports, of which bull fighting remains to be overcome.

In spite of every effort by the Creator, it was never possible to end the practice of sacrifice the Matriarchal fraternity promoted through their collective. [The Inca was one Matriarchal society, the Tibetans another, the Llama reputedly being directly descendant of the Matriarch himself.]

The Matriarchs lost their place as an incarnating force about one hundred and fifty years ago, due to the Matriarch having promoted witch craft among Europeans through the Matriarchal collective. Witches who lived in isolation and poverty, abducted, and ritualistically cannibalised children and adults they found wandering in forests, as the ancient fable of Hansel and Gretel indeed suggests. But in spite of every effort to quell Matriarchy, Matriarchal spirits kept incarnating into each and every society in the world.

Matriarchs do not focus on self outcomes. Instead, they spend their lives trying to hamstring any person who tries to rise above the tide. Matriarchy essentially is about not doing the will of self, and preventing others doing their will. After life, the Matriarchal collective judges spirits on the degree to which they did their duty to the Matriarchal parent. As a result, human society under Matriarchal order quickly sinks into poverty and loss of human dignity as human sacrifice, cannibalism, and the downward drag of Matriarchal insistence on adherence to family order, and social rules, become increasingly oppressive.

The Matriarch gets the feeling that he or she suffers greatly, and almost coincidentally induces the tendency to self sacrifice in others. In past centuries the Matriarch took the support of Matriarchal parents as acknowledgment that karmic debt was owed to the parent. This opened the supportive child to karmic enslavement, a concept I deal with, below.

Matriarchy is not about female or male empowerment. Instead, everyone is seen as equal. In the end, everyone ends up at the bottom of the pile as personal ambition is scorned, and the strong are sacrificed to the self image of the Matriarch.

During Matriarchal ages, daughters need the Matriarch's permission to marry. Typically, one daughter is disadvantaged by the Matriarch refusing permission. This daughter becomes the designated family scape goat.

The family scape goat is the burden bearer for the Matriarchal family's need to be a family. Scapegoats are sexually socialised in such a way that they end up the sacrificial lambs around whose loveless lives their families gather. The scape goat never has a family of her own, and never has sexual relations, by virtue of which she becomes the head of her Matriarchal house, following her life. Should the family scape goat resist emotional control, emotional withdrawal results. When the Matriarch dies, the scape goat usually is left with the family fortune, thereby ensuring family loyalty to her. Here, siblings visit with their children, hoping to inherit.

Depending on their social status, Matriarchs give energy to those who respond to them with love. On the other hand, those who make their disapproval of the Matriarch obvious, or low status people who are above Matriarchs in ability, are held in contempt. Here, the Matriarch holds a negative, anxiety inducing image of the disapproving person in his, or her mind's eye, each time they interact with the disapproving person. For example, the Matriarch may see the disapproving person behind prison bars in his or her mind's eye, or as lying in a sexually compromising position, tied to a bed. This technique is currently widely used by inferior individuals who seek to place themselves above others. Most people in modern society are aware that they sometimes feel uncomfortable, or on the back foot in certain people's presence. This anxiety causes those held in contempt to channel energy to the man, or woman who holds them in contempt. In this way, energy is lost by individuals held in contempt to the collectives of persons holding them in contempt.

During Matriarchal ages, women are not allowed to marry, or have sex again, following divorce, but may do following the death of a husband. Husbands need the Matriarch's permission to divorce, and usually fail to get it. Instead, they usually end up sacrificed at ritualistic seances, which become a plague during Matriarchal ages.

To facilitate Matriarchal supremacy under Matriarchal law, rules quickly come into existence that absolve married women who commit crimes against husbands and children. Paedophilia abounds during Matriarchal ages, and the abandonment of unwanted children after their birth becomes common practice. Ritualistic burial rites upon Matriarchal death centre around shows of sorrow, and remorse for the departure of the Matriarch who is understood to be awaiting the arrival of Matriarchal daughters in the Matriarchal collective. Patriarchal children, identified by astrological charts designed to aid the Matriarch, are designating as so-called 'karmic slaves,' their being earmarked for collection by the Alter Ego, which constitutes 'hell.'

Following the Matriarch's death, the Matriarch does not receive karma for wrongs committed against others, or self. Instead, the Matriarch nominates karmic slaves [usually Patriarchal daughters] to do penance for any wrongs the Matriarch may have committed in her lifetime, including any wrongs the Matriarch committed against the karmic slave herself. This cancels the Matriarch's debt to others, including the karmic slave, leaving the Matriarch free again to incarnate.

During Matriarchal ages, Matriarchs marry more than one husband. Husbands are required to live in the same house, each contributing to the Matriarch's support. Each husband is required to take care of his own child, whom the Matriarch victimizes, should he arrive home later than expected, the Matriarch thereby encouraging his early return from work.

Husbands too, are routinely nominated as karmic slaves during Matriarchal ages, the fourth husband usually being the karmic slave, his usually also serving karma on behalf of the Matriarch, or any family members the Matriarch may care to nominate. During Matriarchal ages the fourth husband was usually a young man the Matriarch married after the age of sixty. As the Matriarch's 'favourite,' he was often the object of the older husbands' jealousy, and fell prey to physical, or sexual retribution.

The Matriarch mediates sexuality during Matriarchal ages, Matriarchal women often suffering from genital insensitivity. They sometimes allow the first husband a concubine, in which case the husband then ends up a karmic slave, his spirit doing penance for the psychological pain caused the Matriarch by the concubine's presence in her husband's life. The Matriarch spends her days and nights morbidly resenting the concubine. Should the concubine conceive, the child is often designated as a karmic slave to the Matriarch, or for ritualistic sacrifice. Often, the Matriarch forfeits the right to the child's being sacrificed. In this case, the child end up as a personal slave to the Matriarch, who often resorts to punishing the child in its mother's presence. As the Patriarch does not allow men to become Matriarchal slaves, Patriarchal collectives do not incarnate during Matriarchal ages. But even during Patriarcal, or Benign ages, the Matriarchal woman often holds the Patriarchal man in contempt. She often nags about shortages in the home, and the Patriarchal husband's frequent late arrival from work. The Patriarchal man, in the presence of this onslaught on his physical freedom, and downward gaze at his confidence, feels a powerful urge to strike out in the face of an anger whose cause he cannot fathom. This often results in sexual violence, and later physical abuse. The reason is that matriarchal women typically see sexuality as payoff for physical support [the crux of Matriarchal male-female value transfers,] while the Patriarch sees sexuality as his right by mere virtue of his having married a woman.

Matriarchs are consciously unaware of their karmic origin during Patriarchal, or Benign ages. During Matriarchal ages however, astrology is quickly resorted to, to discern the deserving from the undeserving. But even during Patriarchal, or Benign ages, Matriarchs are almost intuitively drawn to certain child rearing practices that they cannot explain their affiliation to.

The Matriarch controls by inducing guilt in children. Matriarchs compare children in such a way that all are equal, despite differences. To this end, Matriarchs bath more talented children first, and less talented children, after, in the same water. Here, energy transfer from the more able child to the less able child results in the making over of the less gifted child, often at the cost of both children's individuality. The Patriarchal child is left with a sense of injustice, and embitterment against the parent he or she never can get to the root of.

The Matriarch induces conflict in children, punishing them in ways they cannot connect to the wrongs they supposedly committed, either days later, or in such a way that children cannot make a connection between the transgression, and the punishment inflicted. [Pinching male children's testicles is common practice during Matriarchal ages.]

Matriarchal men's sons routinely fall prey to homosexuality, due to Matriarchal men seeing their Matriarchal spouses, whom they invariably resent, in their sons' eyes. They thus impose the image of the mother, including their resentment of her, on the son, each time they look at him. The need to be had by a man gradually evolves in the child thus violated.

Matriarchs see their children as being of their own social standing. No status the child achieves after, makes any difference to how the Matriarch sees her child. The Matriarch adds her child's achievements to her own, and assumes a position of superiority towards other parents whose children did not achieve as the Matriarch's did.

The Matriarch enforces traditional religion in children, the child often being expected to attend Sunday school alone. This practice, which came into existence in Italy, entailed children being bullied into attending church alone on Sundays, usually against their will. This practice was seen as opening the door for parents to force decisions on children against their will, once children were adults. Seen against the fact that a spirit is judged 'unjust' if it lived a life of not doing its own will, this constituted great evil against children.

Matriarchs are aware that they feel drawn to same-sex company, rather than opposite sex company.

If Matriarchs were left outside in past centuries, following death, they did not accept their fate. Instead, their spirits travelled long distances to reside in their children's homes. At the time of their children's deaths, they tried to attach themselves to a chosen child's spirit to enter the child's spirit's collective. The presence of the Matriarchal spirit was immediately noted by the child's Incarnating spirit, who was unable to disentangle the parent's spirit from the child's. This resulted in both spirits being left out, or collected by the so-called Alter Ego, also known as 'hell,' see 'The Alter Ego,' below.

This absurd paradigm repeatedly swamped the planet, and repeatedly resulted in the planet being destroyed. The first destruction through the removal of the atmosphere occurred about one hundred and twenty thousand years ago, the second at the beginning of the previous age of Aquarius, the third towards the end of the most recent age of Leo, and the fourth, during the age of Taurus. The great flood at the end of the most recent age of Taurus resulted from the atmosphere being selectively withdrawn from areas occupied by Matriarchs. This resulted in prolific rain in some areas, and hardship beyond imagining in other areas, but not extinction.

[Legend has it that the Creator, at the beginning of the most recent age of Taurus had wind that the great spirit Osiris had been sacrificed by the Matriarch. In response, the Creator removed the atmosphere over the areas occupied by the Matriarch. This induced incessant rain in the remaining areas, and permanent changes in weather conditions globally, although the rain cycle was not again compromised. The reason was that Osiris was a 'Man (spirit) who speaks,' and he was killed by a man who was not a 'Man who speaks.' A Man who speaks is a judge of a universe, and, at any time, there is only one per universe. The Creator introduced a rule which stated that a Man who speaks' will never again be killed by a Man who is not a Man who speaks, and that, if this happened again, induction of the sun would follow, and the earth would be destroyed by fire.]

PATRIARCHY

A Patriarch is not a fatherly, or patronising person. Patriarchy [as represented by Islamic male-female value transfers], is a fraternity of male spirits who seek to sacrifice the female spirit to the empowerment of the male spirit. The Patriarchal collective incarnates a man as a woman for reasons of sinfulness, hence the lower status women occupy in Patriarchal societies.

The Patriarch enjoyed a measure of status in past millennia, due to the Creator's having worked with the Patriarch when he returned to earth around thirty thousand years ago to oust Matriarchy, and to begin growing a new kind of man. [No incarnating fraternity is ever allowed to incarnate without the Creator's support, as he alone receives the technology required to create atmosphere, and rain on a desolate planet.]

The Patriarch lost all credibility however, when it became apparent to the Creator that the Patriarchs were in the process of systematically eliminating the giants, spoken about in Genesis 6.

The story of Cain and Abel is the story of what transpired between the Patriarch [Cain], and the giant [Abel], and the God spoken about in that story, was the Creator, see 'Man's Early Evolution,' below.

The Patriarch was incarnated from a great spirit called 'Horus,' and belonged to a fraternity of forty individuals, figure 39. They were given genes by the Creator to upgrade their collective about twenty seven thousand years ago, but were never able to place their collective above other collectives. Following their extermination of Abel, they were ousted from the land of the Creator, which was called 'Egypt' from the beginning of time, 'Eden' having been a dimunitive for 'Egypt.'   Patriarchy never became the Western paradigm. Western Europeans incarnated from the collective of free men since the age of Aries. Patriarchal principles nevertheless influenced Western thought, following Jehovah's taking the place of the Creator as head of the Christian institution around one thousand five hundred years ago. [Jehovah was the Incarnating spirit of the house of Benign Intervention, which combined Patriarchal, and Matriarchal principles since Adam's fall from the Patriarch's grace.]

Through marriage, the Patriarch's wife atones for her husband's wrongs, after life, in return for the physical support she received during her lifetime. To this end, a Patriarchal man and his wife were judged together, following life. This leaves the male spirit free to incarnate again without any time lost. If he had more than one wife, the youngest does penance for his transgressions, while the others' spirits are incarnated as men at the lowest level of consciousness the Patriarchal collective incarnates at.   [The Patriarchal collective incarnates at two levels of consciousness.]

After each lifetime during which a Patriarchal man thus supports a woman, he goes free from blame at the end of his lifetime. After each lifetime a Patriarchal woman spends serving her husband's purpose, and living off his effort, her spirit does penance for wrongs he committed.

The Patriarchal collective strives towards converting all spirits to male spirits. Nevertheless, males who commit transgressions the wife cannot atone for, for example, acts of goodwill towards wives who will not have sex with them, are either destroyed, or given female lifetimes. For this reason, through centuries of incarnation, the Patriarchal male suffers from intuitive fear of emotional involvement with women. He intuitively seeks to have sex with women of low standing as early in his life as possible to build a bulwark against the possibility of his even being attractive to a woman he really could relate to as a human, and a lover.

Patriarchal ideals infiltrated Western society in recent years through the men's movement. The men's movement's favourite hobby horse is the apparent disintegration of marriage, and the corruption of 'Western' values due to sexual freedom, and the availability of contraceptives.

That Western culture is rampant today, and in no danger of being eroded, has apparently evaded these men. That Western values always related to sexual freedom, and standing for personal freedom against forces opposing individual choice, that Western culture never centred around female disempowerment through marriage, and that homosexuality cannot be prevented by forcing men to marry women, and guaranteeing such men employment by excluding women from employment, somehow continues to elude them.

The principles they seek to promote relate to Patriarchal, or Islamic male-female value transfers that have been embraced by a minority group of elderly Western men who feel threatened by older women increasingly seeking out lives of independency, and self realization.

AGE OF DIVISION

During ages of Division, all spirits are incarnated from the collective of 'free men.' No Matriarchal, Patriarchal, or Benign collectives may incarnate during this time. Men and women are judged separately upon entry into the collective, and no spirit receives a female incarnation as punishment. Here, the relative success of each person's individual life is taken as an indication of whether they will contribute to their own evolution in a next lifetime. This alone determines whether or not a next lifetime is given.

Division, as represented by modern Western male-female value transfers, only becomes possible when socio-economic conditions favour personal safety, and freedom from obligation to others. This is the first time in man's history that Division is a real alternative. The paradigm of Division is a possibility that would not have come into existence, had the new Incarnating fraternity not spent the past three hundred years promoting technology, and female equality through the so-called 'Holy Spirit,' an energy channel that spans the universe, spoken about in the gospel of St. John.

Their arrival at the turn of the last century brought immediate, and complete social change over a period of only one hundred years. They immediately triggered two world wars which were closely followed by a massive cultural revolution, whose purpose was to destroy the old order, as represented by royalty who lived off the labour, and tax contributions of men and women they aspired to distance themselves from. Through promoting female equality they endeavoured to quell Patriarchal, and Matriarchal values.

During ages of Division, no spirit pays for the karmic sins of another, and those who follow rules are not as valued as those who learn by their own mistakes. This represents the greatest difference between Division on the one hand, and Patriarchy, Matriarchy, and Benign Intervention, on the other, all of which held that learning by mistakes was the privilege of the gods, and that spirits up to the fourth level of consciousness should learn by following rules.

During ages of Division, souls are not incarnated, and eventual changes in brain structure pave the way for a second spirit to join the first. A state of 'oneness' of two separate spirits from different galaxies, one male, and the other female, in the same body, is symbolised by the double headed eagle, and reflected in the emergence of a new kind of male-female relationship.

BENIGN INTERVENTION
(The Marriage of Ego and Alter Ego)

Benign Intervention originally related to the text book called the 'Kabbalah.'

While Patriarchy represents the sacrifice of the female spirit to the evolution of the male spirit through marriage, Benign Intervention centred around a mastermind relationship between a so-called 'man of the mind,' and a younger individual he trained in the discipline of his trade. The chosen individual sometimes was a childless wife.

The 'man of the mind,' who initiated a project, was labelled the 'ego,' or spirit, in the working relationship. The 'understudy' he worked with, was called the 'alter ego' in the working relationship. Upon entry into the so-called 'higher mansion,' where spirits who achieved outstanding results in their areas of innate talent accrued to following their lives, the two spirits presented themselves as 'ego,' and 'alter ego,' respectively.

For the ego partner, the mastermind existed side by side with marriage during life, but not for the alter ego partner. A man, upon marriage, became an ego, and therefore not eligible as alter ego, or understudy. Similarly, pregnancy excluded women from participating as understudies.

While the wife thus remained the karmic slave of her husband, his alter ego on the other hand, entered the higher mansion with him as a slave spirit, but not a karmic slave. [The Patriarchal karmic slave atoned for the sins of her husband, while the Patriarch's alter ego, or understudy, became a spirit servant in the higher mansion.]

Whether the alter ego was male or female was thus not at issue. The ego partner however, was definitely male, and he sought, through the work that he did, to enter the so-called 'higher mansion' following life, in the presence of an alter ego who would be a spirit servant.

The original arrangement was thus that the alter ego and ego were allowed in together, and that the alter ego partner would place his spirit in service of the ego spirit, as the ego spirit saw fit. However, after a number of alter ego spirits tried to usurp the authority of ego spirits in the higher mansion upon entry, presenting themselves as the ones who effected the outcomes, ego spirits banded together to plot against spirits who entered as alter egos.

Through the Incarnating spirit of the higher mansion incarnating himself as a Greek, the culture of homosexuality among intellectual men came into existence. This man formed an organisation for men who sought to work in partnerships with other men. He told all those who joined his organization about the possibility that they could be usurped in the higher mansion by their understudies. To combat the possibility of this happening, ego men were encouraged to have homosexual relationships with their understudies.

A spirit is a 'man,' and a man does his will. Anal sexuality presupposes submission to imposition by another. Submitting himself to another's will immediately renders a spirit an 'alter ego,' and thus ineligible for collection by any collective, other than either the Alter Ego ['hell'], or the higher mansion as a servant spirit. The reason was that spirit energy carries genetic information, as body cells carry genetic information, and that during anal intercourse, energy transfer occurs from the imposing partner to the imposed upon partner.

By the time they entered the higher mansion, the energy similarity between the spirit energy of the ego partner, and alter ego partner was so great that the ego spirit was able to consume the spirit of the alter ego. This amounted to the life, and the ability of the alter ego spirit being given the ego spirit, and the alter ego spirit disappearing as a separate entity in the way illustrated below, in the story of the judgment of a man called 'Ani,' and his wife, named 'Thuthu.' [Genetic similarity could also result from energy transfer from a woman to a man under her auspices. Here, the man was similarly rendered the alter ego partner of the woman, for which his spirit was summarily destroyed, following judgment.]

Should both men have sexually, or emotionally imposed

themselves on one another, neither would have been accepted by either their respective Incarnating spirit houses, or by the higher mansion. Here, both spirits would have been collected by the Alter Ego, or left outside.

Homosexuality in Ancient Greece thus came about as the result of a nasty little plot by those who initiated projects to ensure their acceptance into the higher mansion above those on whose services their success invariably depended. This, as most political plots, was never known to those sacrificed, but only to those who sought to mount themselves on top of the abilities of those they then sought to consider below them.

Imagine the horror of a spirit discovering, following life, that, after a lifetime of work, contributing to a project, and his total dedication to earning his boss' goodwill, that his dedication to another's cause had rendered their spirit good enough only for consumption by another spirit, or in 'hell.' This spirit failed to see that he could work for an independent living, and that he did not need to get sexually involved with another person to realize his goals. This spirit unwittingly rendered himself a soul through his implicit agreement to support another reach his aim, and then an alter ego by his agreement to subject his will to that of another by agreeing to sacrifice his sexuality to another's need for a karmic servant. [My best sources have it that, when all is said and done, anal sexuality does not amount to sexuality., but rather to stimulation of the genital area to mediate the shock of anal entry.]

It was deemed by the ancients that a time would come during which women would be unwilling to assume the status of either soul, or alter ego to men, in spite of their having been socialised, as ancient women were, to assume such roles. Once this happened, it was deemed, man would return to the law given man at the beginning of time: that God and man would live   together, see 'Understanding Revelations.'

To be able to escalate one's own rate of evolution, and to understand how to make a lifetime count in terms of spirit outcomes, it is imperative one understands how each aspect of the human psyche contributes to either advantage, or disadvantage life outcomes. To thtis end, I shall refer to the story of the judgment of the spirit of a man called 'Ani,' who lived during an era of Benign Intervention, possibly at the fifth level of consciousness, as the spirits undergoing judgment were astral spirits, and not 'soft' spirits. [An astral spirit is a calcium frame that follows the form of a human body. The 'soft' spirit has less cohesion, and appears rather as a human-like energy form, ranging from pink to white. Pink and yellow spirits are called souls, and they accrue to the house of the Patriarch, and the house of souls, respectively.]

Before continuing, it is necessary to understand that each person belongs to a spirit house to which his or her spirit returns, following life, 'Then Abraham gave up the ghost ... and was gathered to his people' (Genesis 25:8). Secondly, it is to be understood that physical relatedness does not necessarily indicate spiritual relatedness, 'And die in the mount ... and be gathered unto thy people ... as Aaron thy brother ... was gathered unto his people' (Deuteronomy 32:50).

Figure 7   portrays Osiris sitting in his shrine. A shrine is a space occupied by the energy of a great spirit. The great spirit contains his energy within the confines of this space by erecting energy screens around his place of work, figure 7.

Osiris was the Incarnating spirit during the most recent age of Leo. He was the god of the dead, or the god of the house of souls. [The house of souls is known as 'the house of the dead,' while the house of spirits is known as 'the house of the living,' During ages of Division, only the house of spirits incarnates.] During the age of Leo, the god of the house of the dead was the Incarnating spirit.

Behind Osiris were Isis and Nephthys, his twin soul, figure 7. After the age of Taurus, the soul on the left [genetically determined], was commonly taken to relate to the house of the alter ego, while the soul on the right was commonly taken to relate to the house of souls. In cases of alter ego overlay, due to authoritarian parental jealousy or vindictiveness, the left soul allowed itself to be sacrificed.

Following life, a spirit returns to the spirit collective where the degree of growth in consciousness it achieved during its lifetime is assessed. In past centuries karma was meted out in such a way that a spirit's weaknesses were escalated, to keep humans at a g iven level of consciousness.

During ages of Division the reason for the individual lifetime is that the spirit should grow by doing its will. Growth in consciousness is achieved by overcoming psychological, and physical obstacles that come in the way of a person's determination to succeed at earning a living by doing his assigned work.

WHAT IS A SPIRIT?

A spirit is an energy person with consciousness. At the fifth level of consciousness, the spirit evolves an astral body, figure 8. At lower levels of consciousness the spirit takes a more or less

30

human appearance, depending on the density of its energy.

Prior to a child's birth, the spirit destined to attach to the child, hangs around the mother. Following birth, it attaches to the child's body. Should there be an imposing spirit in the home, trying to incarnate itself by overlaying the infant before the designated spirit arrives, the designated spirit calls the Incarnating spirit upon its arrival in the mother's vicinity. [The imposing spirit usually attempts to enter the child's body while the child is in the mother's womb.] In such cases the Incarnating spirit arrives to remove the imposing spirit.

Historical evidence of spirits connecting to people at birth, can be found in Genesis in the story of the births of Rebecca's two children, Jacob and Esau, 'After that [Esau's birth] came his brother [Jacob] out, and his [Jacob's] hand took hold on Esau's heel.' Obviously, this relation cannot pertain to physical birthing dynamics. It is not logical to think that one baby grabbed the other's heel. It firstly would have lacked the necessary co-ordination, and secondly, the required hand size. In addition, a baby could not yet understand the symbolic meaning of this gesture, but a spirit attaching to the baby can, and in this case, did. To grab someone by the heel is to accuse him or her of violating the conditions of a contract that preceded incarnation.

A pure human spirit's energy cannot be seen under aura imaging, as it is white. When it is alter-ego contaminated, it has a purple hue. Purple is a colour that was traditionally incorrectly assumed to relate to spirituality when in fact it relates to the Alter Ego. White-pink is associated with consciousness, light blue with frozen emotion, dark blue with authority, while green relates to healing. Soul energy can easily be observed about the body.

It varies in colour, pink and yellow being the most common. Pink is associated with permeability, yellow relates to conscious functioning, while white relates to spirituality, see 'How to Make Yourself a Man.'

Spirits should call on their spirit collectives following life, as the Alter Ego poses an ongoing threat to spirits awaiting collection. If a spirit is not gathered back into its spirit house following life, its energy begins dissipating due to atmospheric, and weather conditions impacting it. Water is particularly destructive to an unsheltered spirit in the longer term, although damp sustains a spirit. As it becomes increasingly diffuse, due to its not being supported by the collective's energy, and due to its being exposed to the elements, or household chemicals, it becomes increasingly diffuse, until it loses all its energy, and cannot move at all.

The soul channels its energy to the spirit upon death. This enables the spirit to free itself from the body. Following Ani's lifetime, his body was left behind in his tomb, while his 'house of spirits' hovered overhead, waiting to guide his spirit to the Hall of Judgment, figure 9. As he entered the Hall of Judgment, he was followed by his wife, Thuthu, figure 10.

At a glance, two things were apparent. Firstly, Ani and Thuthu were of high birth, and secondly, Ani's spirit did not do its will during its lifetime.

A spirit who does its will is masculine in countenance, even if it is the spirit of a woman. Ani's spirit was visibly effeminate, although not quite as effeminate as Thuthu's. The feminine appearance does not indicate effeminate inclination at the physical level, neither does it visibly affect the appearance of the body. The feminine appearance only indicates that a spirit does the will of another. A spirit who supports another at the cost of doing its own will, and work, is called a soul. A spirit who does the will of another, is an alter ego, and has a rigid, and aged appearance. A soul's will is to support another. An alter ego's will is to do another's will, while an evil eye imposes a pradigm previously imposed on it, on others.

The spirit grows in masculine countenance, and grows a penis when it does its own will. The penis indicates a spirit's inclination to do its own will. Such a spirit can hold more than one occupation, or diversify business interests, for example. Whether or not a penis exists, is sometimes indicated during dream sleep after the age of forty five, usually in the presence of a great spirit.

A spirit doing its will relates to that spirit fulfilling the contract it entered with its Incarnating spirit before life. This spirit strives to overcome limitations, and longs to enjoy the life experience. A spirit who spends its life seeking to control other people in one way or the other accrues to the collective of the Patriarch following life, and is made an evil eye as Thuthu's spirit indeed was.

The major difference between the masculine, and relatively feminine spirit is that the masculine spirit is pleased with whom it is. If it incarnates as a woman it is feminine, and loves being a woman. If it incarnates as a man, it similarly loves being a man. It knows what it is about, and sets about trying to find out what it is supposed to do. The masculine spirit tends to give the body a well shaped masculine, or feminine figure in clothing.

The effeminate spirit, by contrast, is dissatisfied with whom it is, and typically wishes he or she were something, or someone different. It may be dissatisfied being male, being female, being fat, being thin, being blonde, being rich, being poor, having a job, not having a job, and so on.

Homosexuality does not relate to masculinity, or femininity

at the spirit level. Instead, it relates to a child having the image of his opposite sex parent imposed on his mind's eye by his same-sex parent. Whether the homosexual man or woman wants to impose his sexuality on another, or be imposed on, relates to character difference, and the intention of the parent who thus destroyed his innate sense of self.

WHAT IS A SPIRIT HOUSE?

A spirit house is a small spirit collective that lives within a larger collective. The spirit house is symbolised by a tree, and is headed by a 'cosmic mother,' figure 11.

A spirit house is given permission to incarnate spirits under the directive of the Incarnating spirit who presides over the spirit collective. By successfully incarnating spirits, the spirit house tries to rise in status in the pyramidal hierarchy of the collective of which it is part. The spirit house avoids taking unnecessary risks when incarnating spirits, as one person injuring another indebts his spirit house to the spirit house of the injured party. This results in the indebted spirit house having to forfeit energy to the injured spirit house.

The ultimate aim of every incarnating spirit is to maximise its growth in consciousness over successive lifetimes. To this end, the cosmic mother incarnates as many spirits as she has guardian angels to oversee. Most spirit houses only have one guardian angel, but some have as many as two or three. The biggest Incarnating house has four thousand five hundred angels at its command.

WHAT IS A SPIRIT COLLECTIVE?

A spirit collective is a collection of spirits at the same level of consciousness who share commonality of genetic information. A spirit collective effectively is a 'gathering of minds,' and, as can be imagined, when many minds meet, a collective 'character' comes into existence. While the collective appears as an energy cloud, its character may be symbolised by a face, or archetype, figure 12. A collective is not a cloud blanket that covers the whole earth's surface. Rather, a collective appears as an energy 'ribbon' which moves dynamically, except for collectives that are lower in energy that just hang about. To maximise diversity in consciousness evolution, each spirit house is assigned a specific evolutionary growth path along the lines of which each spirit it incarnates grows in consciousness. This means that spirits who incarnate from the same spirit house all grow through negotiating similar obstacles that are placed in their way to success, in addition to their incarnating under similar astrological influences.

By overcoming the specific obstacles to success placed before it, each spirit incarnated by a spirit house grows in tenacity, and understanding of the law of cause and effect, that is, understanding about which actions are likely to produce which outcomes under which circumstances. There is a direct relationship between rewards at the end of a lifetime and the extent to which a spirit delivered on its agreed life work, however simple or complex that work might have been.

A spirit collective usually incarnates until it reaches the evolutionary goals it envisaged at the beginning of its time. This may take anything from one age to a maximum of twelve ages to achieve. Hereafter, the collective has to leave the earth plane, unless it is the highest collective, in which case it needs to be joined by a new Incarnating fraternity, which results in a new human experience emerging.

WHAT IS CONSCIOUSNESS?

Consciousness is not an absolute term. One does not either have it, nor not. Consciousness is spread over a continuum ranging from less conscious to more conscious.

Consciousness is insight into which actions are likely to produce which outcomes under which circumstances. Consciousness also relates to power, and power relates to the ability to be your own man. To be your own man is to live for your own sake.

Some actions can be left behind. However, some choices compromise the spirit's ability to be recollected into its spirit collective. Such actions constitute cardinal sin. Cardinal sin relates to action that renders the spirit unable to fulfil its life mission. If the spirit tried to resist such action, and if its wisdom was overridden by mind set, or feelings of obligation to others, the spirit sometimes tries to leave the body without compromising the soul's ability to continue life. Depending on the soul's strength, temporary paralysis of the extremities may follow that may become permanent. In this case, the person may become far more susceptible to disease than before, much as children are more susceptible to disease than adults, prior to their spirits receiving additional layers of energy from the Incarnating spirit, after age nine. Should the spirit have consumed the soul during life, coma results.

On the earth plane at present, four levels of consciousness exist. Although social learning plays a determining role in growth in consciousness, genetic influences play a deciding role in what is learned. In other words, genetic influences determine the direction in which consciousness evolves. Alter ego values favour consciousness about rights to take decisions others end up paying the cost of, and feelings of entitlement.

Returning again now to Ani entering the Hall of Judgment, followed by his wife 'Thuthu,' the objective appearance of Ani's spirit having been taken into account, his spirit [symbolised by a feather], was weighed against his soul [which was Thuthu's spirit, which was symbolised by a terra cotta face], while his 'house of spirits' was perched against the wall, looking on, figures 13, and 14.

The reason why the soul was symbolised by a terra cotta face [the most basic earth element], was that the face represented the soul, and that the soul related to the physical life experience. The spirit, on the other hand, was symbolised by a feather. Spirituality is associated with high mindedness, which in turn is associated with weightlessness, and independency from physical dynamics.

By weighing the soul against the feather, the relative level of high mindedness of the soul was assessed. In other words, the level of consciousness of Thuthu's spirit [considered Ani's soul for purposes of judgment], was compared to that of Ani's spirit. A spirit's level of evolution relates to the degree to which it inclines to focus on achieving self outcomes, as opposed to supporting others in their quest for self realization, or imposing on others.

The idea behind the weighing was thus to see which spirit was more high minded, and which spirit had been the soul in

37

the relationship. If the spirit weighed more than the soul, the spirit was deemed to have been the soul in the relationship. In such a case, the husband was devoured by the 'Devourer of the Unjust,' for incorrectly presenting himself as the spirit, or ego, upon entry, figure 15.

The meaning of marriage was that the wife's spirit would become the husband's soul upon their entry into the husband's spirit collective during ages of Patriarchy, or Benign Intervention. Thuthu's spirit, due to its having been Ani's wife, would thus have been judged as Ani's soul. Should Thuthu have been Ani's understudy, she would also have been judged as his alter ego.

The concepts of soul, and alter ego respectively, relate to consciousness. A soul wants to support a spirit doing his will. [A spirit who does his will is called 'man,' even when it is in the body of a woman.] An alter ego does the will of another. The alter ego shadows the spirit, is authoritarian by nature, and is what the spirit is not. Souls accrue to the house of the Matriarch following life, while alter egos accrue to the house of the Alter Ego.

That Thuthu indeed considered herself Ani's alter ego was indicated by Thuthu's carrying an ankh in her right hand as she entered the Hall of Judgment, identifying herself as alter ego, figure 10. That Thuthu's spirit was judged as both Ani's alter ego, and his soul, is indicated by the presence of both a clay face, and a tongue in the Hall of Judgment, see 'The Alter Ego,' below.

THE ALTER EGO

The colour of energy depends on its frequency, and amplitude. The colour depends on emotional factors, and in the

38

human energy system the psyche vibrates to the frequency of its colour. As emotional factors change, the colour of the psyche changes, the psyche's vibration spirals up or down, and observable behaviour changes accordingly. Behaviour, and consciousness are thus dependent on two factors: conscious control, and energy frequency and amplitude.

An alter ego is a spirit that is purple in colour. While the spirit does its work, and while the soul supports, the alter ego is not focussed on work, nor does it support, but subtly opposes. While the soul in the Hall of Judgment was therefore symbolised by the terra cotta face, the alter ego was symbolised by the tongue.

The tongue has long been associated with the alter ego, and with speaking loosely about intimate matters. Alter ego behaviour relates to nagging, speaking about sensitive matters as if they were trivial issues, scandalising people, living off the efforts of others, or the alter ego spirit imposing his or her will on others.

To judge the alter ego's level of evil, that is, the degree to which it opposed the spirit doings its will, the tongue's energy was channelled into the foot of a female baboon, figure 16. This changed the frequency at which the baboon's energy field vibrated. The female baboon's change in behaviour under the influence of the incoming energy frequency was observed. To the extent that the baboon spoke compulsively about sensitive matters that could embarrass the spirit, the alter ego was taken to have been more or less evil, and the spirit's level of resolve to succeed against the obstacle that the alter ego posed, was assessed.

Although it may seem impossible that the baboon's behaviour would not change under the influence of the alter ego's energy, many people routinely find themselves in the company of people in whose presence they behave uncharacteristically.

Most people have found themselves becoming 'rough around the edges' in some people's company. Most use more socially unacceptable words, speak out of turn, reveal information about friends they normally would keep confidential, and so on. After, they may feel regretful of their behaviour, but fail to understand why they acted as they did.

In such cases, they acted under the influence of alter ego energy. Alter Ego people tend to give energy. Receiving energy feels rewarding to a spirit at first. Alter Ego energy entering a spirit's energy field spirals down the receiving spirit's energy frequency, and amplitude.

At the conscious level, the energy recipient feels important, as if goodwill [affection not related to sexual interest,] is communicated to him, or her. After some time, as the energy received begins to decay in the energy field of the receiver, the receiver begins to feel dirty, and vaguely anxious.

The question arises as to why the alter ego's energy was channelled into the foot of a female baboon, and not any other animal's? The female baboon represents the lowest level of consciousness found in any female primate. Females routinely abuse youngsters, bully one another, and hold out youngsters as protection against male abuse when presenting themselves for impregnation.

The quality of energy forced into the baboon's energy field sometimes caused the baboon to reveal sensitive secrets about the spirit. The alter ego lies often, but also speaks the truth, often out of turn, and often in an ill advised manner.

Having observed the baboon's reaction, Anubis [the devil at the time], and the Incarnating spirit of the house of the alter ego during ages of Benign Intervention, used information gleaned from the baboon's reaction to the tongue's energy to try to 'trick' spirits into confessing to transgressions committed.   [Anubis had the appearance of a Jackal-like animal.   His appearance symbolised cunning, as   he used cunning to trick spirits into confessing to transgressions during life.]

It was usually on the alter ego's accusations about the spirit that Anubis questioned the spirit until confirmation of would-be transgressions could either be obtained, or not, and, it was on the appearance of the baboon under the influence of alter ego energy channelled into it, that the identity of persons who overlaid the spirit receiving judgment was determined.

Absolute rejection of accusations was required to escape punishment due to alter ego indiscretions. Spirits needed to negate all   accusations directed at them.   In this way hypocrisy was escalated during ages of Patriarchy, Matriarchy, and Benign Intervention.   During times of Division on the other hand, no such trickery is used. The focus is on helping the spirit grow, and not on retribution.

Following the recording of Ani's judgment by Thoth [who compared what was given out against what was received back, figure 15,] Thuthu's spirit channelled its energy to Ani's spirit, figure 17, see 'The Meaning of Marriage,' below.

The presence of Thuthu's spirit in Ani's spirit, following Thuthu's and Ani's spirits having become one, is indicated by the change in appearance in Ani's dress, upon his exiting the Hall of Judgment with Horus, figures 18, and 17.   The lines on Ani's spirit indicate places in the body where the soul connects to the spirit in life, and where both connect to the physical energy cen- tres. The spirit primarily anchors in the spleen, from where it connects to other nerve ends.

Spirits appear as clothed human figures as spirit naked-ness symbolises sexual abuse at the time of death. The evolved spirit 'clothes' itself, as it sees appropriate. 'Clothing' most often chosen by spirits are garments worn at the time of death, or during the most significant event in the spirit's life, such events relating either to a major achievement, or to the time of the body's demise. At the fifth level of consciousness, the astral spirit appears as a human being. At this level of consciousness, the astral spirit's energy is so dense that it virtually is a calcium frame, which appears as a fully clothed person.

Where people are deemed to have caused their own deaths, their spirits are left in the fifth dimension, or 'eternal dark' that exists within the ether. [Suicide is not implicated here as much as irrespon-sible actions that lead to accidents, or violent death.] By agreement with the Incarnating spirit, spirits who are deemed to have con-tributed to the ending of their lives, re-enact the drama that preceded their demise each time the astronomical influences are the same as they were at the time of the spirits' acting against their own best inter-est. If astronomical influences were general, the dramas are reenacted often, while less general astronomical conditions result in infrequent appearances of spirits.

Turning now to Ani sitting before Osiris, figure 21, it is pos-sible to see Thuthu's energy being conducted from Ani's spirit to Osiris' shrine. It is clear that single leafs of spirit energy were rising through the stack before Osiris to be suspended from Osiris' lower self. [As can be seen, one spirit layer, or spirit 'leaf,' was already suspended behind Isis and Nephthys, figure 19.] As the energy layer rose before Osiris, it was imbued with karma for its next life-time. This effectively means that Osiris imposed his will for each spirit leaf on that spirit leaf as it passed before him.

THE EVIL EYE

The right eye of the body belongs to the soul. The mind's eye belongs to the spirit. An eyebrow can be seen peeping over the shoulder of the Patriarch's higher self, figure 20. As can be seen, this is a left brow.

If a soul, or spirit becomes 'programmed' to do the will of others, it is deemed an alter ego. If an alter ego becomes programmed to accept traditional male-female value transfers, that alter ego becomes an evil eye, and the left eye is shared between soul, and alter ego. [It is important to note that the left spirit is genetically determined. The right soul, however, is given at the second level of consciousness, and the right soul relates to the right brain hemisphere, and thus to the left eye of the body. Should the right soul, which is the spirit at the first level of consciousness, be contaminated in the way Thuthu's spirit leafs were, such a person's left eye continually delivers the message imposed on his, or her spirit prior to their incarnation, to others, fig. 22.]

In addition to being programmed in the collective, a spirit can be rendered an evil eye by authoritarian parents who impose rigid traditional male-female values on their children, especially values relating to female virtue.

Some collectives only incarnate spirits who are evil eyes. If a spirit who is not an evil eye is incarnated by such a collective, the spirit is first made an evil eye. This happened to Thuthu's spirit. One such collective is the house of the Patriarch. The Evil Eye is a Patriarchal collective of male spirits who look to inhibit confident self expression in women. The whole of the Patriarch is about eclipsing the female principle.

The message behind an evil eye is 'pulsated' outward, projected by energy supplied by the physical brain of the person whose spirit is an evil eye, to the higher minds of any persons who find themselves in the presence of a person who is an 'evil eye.'

An evil eye is thus a man or a woman who wishes to impose an image, previously imposed on their spirits, on others. Such people's eyes seem 'hard,' and people born from the collective of 'free men' feel mild anxiety in their presence. 'Evil eyes' are unaware at the conscious level that their eyes speak a subliminal message into the eyes of others. To such people, power women seem threatening, and power men who support female independency are seen as weak. [Legend has it that, should the subconscious mind receive the message behind an evil eye six hundred times, a bell tolls in the fifth dimension, sometimes audibly heard, to announce that a particular conscious mind had opened his spirit to receiving an imposing point of view so many times that he or she accepted the message behind the evil eye, and thus lost his, or her place in his or her spirit collective.]   The unspoken messages behind evil eyes are not understood by the conscious minds of those their messages are   directed at, but only by their subconscious minds.

As can be seen, the house of the Patriarch was literally snowed under with evil eyes, figure 23. Each time the alter ego behind the falcon delivered its message to the falcon, a leaf of energy split away from it, and fell on the house of spirits of the Patriarch.

Working with the house of the Patriarch, some of the evil eyes transferred to Osiris' dress, from where they transferred into the spirits Osiris was in the process of imbuing with karma. In this way, each spirit was made an evil eye to incarnate already 'naturally' inclined to deliver the message each Patriarchal spirit conveys to all women, even to women born from the collective of 'free men,' 'I am above you,' in spite of the Patriarchal, and Matriarchal collectives being the lowest spirit collectives.

During ages of Division, souls are not incarnated, and changes in brain structure open the psyche to receiving a 'twin spirit' later in life. This obviates the necessity for one spirit to consume another before it is able to incarnate at a higher level of consciousness, and at the physical level, the twin spirit opens the psyche to the arrival of the 'spirit mate' relationship. This is a sexual relationship that enables each person to connect with his, or her highest good.

UNDERSTANDING KARMA

As Thuthu's energy was being channelled from Ani to Osiris, Ani held in his hand what appeared to be a small sheath of wheat, figure 24. Connecting the body to the spirit at the naval, are transparent spaghetti-like energy 'tubes,' one may think of as sheaths of energy on which information about the circumstances of a person's life is digitally stored. Following life, these energy tubes are gathered like sheaths of wheat, and broken off, so that their contents may be scrutinized.

The ego partner's spirit [Ani in this case,] during ages of Patriarchy, and Benign Intervention, was not judged for wrongs committed against others. Instead, the wife stood in for any wrongs the spirit of the husband may have committed during the lifetime lived. The husband's spirit was only punished for subjecting himself to authority other than Patriarchal authority.

To gain access to the information digitally inscribed on the spirit throughout life, the energy of the spirit was run over a low ampere rod, through what appears to be a lamp, whose function was to amplify the colour, and thus the level of consciousness of the spirit-energy flowing through it, figure 25.

As the energy moved over the rod towards the lamp, a three dimensional image of the contents of the information inscribed on the energy sheaths appeared above the rod for all to see.

Above the rod before Ani, a duck with its wings broken off was displayed, figure 24. A duck symbolically represents a man, while broken wings symbolise a broken spirit, that is, a spirit that split off a part of itself to avoid the whole of it being contaminated by a leaf of alter ego energy projected towards it during circumstances of emotional upheaval, by a person born from an alter ego collective The spirit is symbolised by a feather. For this reason, the event of the spirit splitting off part of itself is symbolised by two smaller feathers, figure 26.   Energy overlays are usually received from marriage partners, grandparents, parents or strangers the overlaid person allowed to discipline them.

Spirits incarnated from lower levels of consciousness sometimes try to piggy back into collectives that incarnate at higher levels of consciousness by overlaying spirits of 'high birth' while such spirits are children or young adults, see 'Karmic Contracts,' below. Once broken, a spirit does not do its will, but the will of the person who overlaid him, or her to prevent further overlay. [Psychic overlays contain 'energy parasites' that draw energy from the spirit, much as physical parasites draw energy from the body.]

As a spirit's integrity is destroyed by invading energy overlays, broken spirits feel feelings of animosity towards those who overlaid them. The alter ego overlay on the other hand, feels feelings of goodwill towards the person it originally was part of. Ambivalent feelings towards those who violated them, are thus common in abused individuals. The extent of their subconscious fear of those who overlaid them, is only ever experienced by people when they confront those who overlaid them.

Once their spirits are broken, people begin to focus on controlling others. Focus on self outcomes lose its importance, as the overlaid individual's spirit withdraws to protect itself from further overlays. Depending on his or her character, overlaid individuals either seek to move away from overlaying people, or to please, or to overlay, in turn. [I explore the overlays Ani received from Thuthu, and the Matriarch, and how it affected outcomes for both spirits after their lives, below.]

THE HIGHER MIND

Below the small stack before Ani, to the left of the yellow lamp, a thicker bundle of energy sheaths can be seen, figure 24. They connect the house of spirits to the higher mind, and they represent the proverbial 'hair on your head' that is counted, figure 31. Depending on the individual's level of consciousness, he or she has either more, or less 'hair.' As with the sheaths in Ani's hand, the sheaths from his head were gathered by Horus, and broken off.

Ani's higher mind was symbolically represented by the small pink 'bubble' above his head, figure 32. The higher mind contains 'karma,' which influences the direction of relationships between the individual, and people the individual meets in his or her life, which further influences life choices and outcomes.

[Karma relates to wrongs that were committed against an individual by significant others during previous lifetimes. Its presence in the higher mind potentially enables an individual to repay in a present lifetime what went wrong in a past lifetime, or to overcome destructive tendencies.]

The contents of Ani's higher mind was symbolically represented by the contents of the large stack above his head. In other words, what was symbolically inserted below the little pink cap on Ani's head was displayed above his head.

At the fourth level of evolution the higher mind appears as a white-pink energy field about one inch above the head, about the size of a golf ball. The higher mind contains up to seven lifetimes' karma, each level of the stack representing one lifetime. If karma relating to any one lifetime is not balanced within seven years of that lifetime, the spirit's life is given to others, as Thuthu's indeed was.

During his first lifetime, Ani married two women, and in each case, the marriage was not consummated, figure 34. Turning now to figure 33, it emerges that, during that same lifetime, Ani's higher mind was overlaid by energy leafs from four different individuals. This means that the spirit collectives to which those individuals belonged received energy from Ani's brain, in place of Ani's spirit house. Losing energy from the brain results in lowered intelligence, headaches, tiredness, lack of energy, and depression.

During his next lifetime, Ani found himself at the receiving end of a mother who was a so-called 'evil eye,' figure 35. [An evil eye tells people that they are below the evil eye.] People who are evil eyes belong to Patriarchal collectives. Evil eyes are authoritarian, and do not think that women have the same right to enjoyment as men. As a result of his involvement with a mother who was an evil eye, Ani himself became an evil eye during his second lifetime, figure 35. Considering the karma Ani received following two successive lifetimes, it is clear that, during each lifetime, he failed to succeed as a result of others emotionally violating him.

An energy overlay is a piece, or leaf of psychic energy with consciousness, and intention. The intention an energy overlay carries is the intention the sender has for the receiver.

Energy can only move from one person to another in circumstances of emotional upheaval. An energy overlay has the power to change the consciousness of the receiver in such a way that the receiver begins to serve the purpose of the sender of the energy overlay, as the overlay gains control over one or the other mental faculty of the receiver.

During his third lifetime [for which he was in the process of receiving judgment,] Ani again fell prey to energy overlay. Here he was enslaved by a woman of high birth, almost certainly Thuthu, figure 26.

Having been rendered an evil eye during his second lifetime, that is, a man who looks at others with a view to imposing an image on them, that he was programmed to impose on them, he married a woman born from the collective of the Matriarch. Having received a third lifetime to correct what had happened before, Ani became enslaved by Thuthu from the point of view of the Incarnating fraternity which upheld the principles of Benign Intervention. [Benign Intervention applied Patriarchal rules when judging men, and Matriarchal rules when judging women. By arrangement between the Matriarch, and the Patriarch during the age of Taurus, men were generally considered Patriarchal spirits, hence the association between being male, and Patriarchy.]

From the point of view of Benign Intervention, which came into effect immediately after the Matriarch was again allowed to join the Incarnating fraternity, in spite of their having laid the planet waste prior to the last age of Aquarius, Ani was rendered a sex slave. A sex slave from the Patriarchal perspective, was a man who remained faithful to only one wife, in spite of her refusing to be impregnated by him. The point here was to discourage men falling prey to emotional involvement with women.

By contrast, the Matriarch discouraged unwanted pregnancies under Matriarchal law. The Matriarch expected husbands to be disciplined when having sex with wives, but not concubines. An instrument of cruelty was used to thrash men on the buttocks for failing to exercise the expected level of discipline. The wife accusing her husband brought a team of Matriarchal police upon the husband, and punishment was administered as recently as Greek times, which left higher class women high and dry at their homes, while the men had sex with one another in the spa's of the day.

As a result of his subjecting himself to Matriarchal discipline, Ani's sexual centres were overlaid by an energy overlay whose intention was to encourage him to have sex in a contraceptive way. The presence of a man during the time of Ani's punishment is certain, as he received a male energy overlay. The overlay pertained to male sexuality, and it overlaid the creation of offspring.

As a result of the overlay Ani received during punishment, Ani's karma relating to offspring was blocked, and none of the three children his spirit agreed to have, were born, figure 27.

Further energy overlays Ani received from Thuthu lodged between the two parts his spirit split into, as a result of the punishment he agreed to undergo. This silenced his spirit forever, figure

29. This kind of overlay causes the conscious mind to identify with the value system of the individual who inflicted the pain, to prevent further overlay. The clear part of spirit energy recedes, so that the wisdom of the spirit, and its reason for incarnating are forever lost to the subconscious mind. [This is what it is to be split down the middle.]

The crow [figure 28] symbolises the Matriarch. This symbol indicates that Ani was at the mercy of a Matriarchal person who asked, and demanded, but never gave anything in return.

The rule under Patriarchy, and Benign Intervention, from the Patriarchal point of view, was that an impotent man had to get divorced from his wife, who was seen as the reason for his impotence. A man's obligation was to reproduce. Ani failed to do this, and instead received energy overlays from Thuthu and the Matriarchal fraternity, rendering his spirit vulnerable to collection by her spirit. In spite of the fact that he never again had heterosexual sex with her, following his flogging, he remained married to her, and faithful to her.

All indications are that Thuthu held on to Matriarchy, so that, by the end of their lives together, Ani had come under Thuthu's auspices, and both had come under the auspices of the Matriarch, figure 30.

At the entrance to the Patriarchal Hall of Judgment, Thuthu waited for Ani who went before as the ego, while Thuthu went behind as the alter ego. During judgment however, it was found that Ani had in fact been an alter ego to have done Thuthu's will to remain childless. It was therefore determined that Ani's spirit would be destroyed by the so-called 'Devourer of the Unjust,' figure 15. [As can be seen, the

Devourer of the Unjust had a spider under its arm. The arm pit symbolises sexuality, and a spider under the arm is thus a curse that symbolically renders a spirit sexually unappealing, even when in an attractive body, see 'The Concept of Curse,' below.]

Ani lost his life, that is, his right to incarnate, through his tendency to support others in their needs to impose their will on him. Thuthu's spirit, who was found menacing in its determination to do its will at the cost of others, was leafed, and programmed as evil eyes to be incarnated by the house of the Patriarch. Men born from the Patriarchal collective incarnate ready programmed to understand the rights of the Patriarch in the family equation, to do the will of those who represent the Patriarchal order, and to give women a clear message regarding their place in the Patriarchal scheme of things!

In summary, it can thus be said that a spirit is an energy entity that does its will, while allowing others to do theirs. A soul is a spirit who lost its status as a spirit through its tendency to support other spirits doing their will at the cost of its doing its own will. An alter ego is a spirit who lost its status as a soul due to its doing the will of others. An evil eye is a spirit who lost its status as an alter ego through its authoritarian tendency to impose an ideology previously imposed on it, on others.

Life in past centuries was simplistic. People did not receive complex karma. Life centred around procreation, and working to support the physical livelihood of self, and a family. Personal fulfilment was never a human issue before the onset of the age of Aquarius. Not producing children in those days constituted failure in delivering on the spirit's agreement with the universe, which amounted to cardinal sin. Thuthu was found to have been an alter ego, and hence her spirit was given to the house of the Patriarch as seven alter ego spirits to be programmed as evil eyes, and incarnated as evil eyes at the lowest levels of consciousness the Patriarchal collective incarnated at. In this way, life was proliferated at the lower end of the consciousness ladder since the beginning of time.

After the seventh lifetime during which a spirit supported another doing his or her will at the cost of the spirit doing his or her own will, the spirit was given to the house of souls, from where it was incarnated as a woman to support someone else's life. In this way, the woman's image during ages of Benign Intervention became associated with marriage, and child rearing to the exclusion of any form of work.

During ages of Division, twin souls are not given, as the twin spirit is given once human consciousness reaches the correct level of maturity, usually after age forty five, see 'Understanding Revelations.'

Ani lost his incarnation after only three successive lifetimes, due to his having been sexually enslaved by a woman from the point of view of Benign Intervention, as I already mentioned. Ani was a man, and married under Patriarchal law. Instead of upholding Patriarchal law in his life, he instead fell prey to his wife's Matriarchal rights to refuse to be impregnated unless she agreed, a right Patriarchy does not acknowledge. Benign Intervention considered Thuthu an alter ego. The onus was thus on Ani to take the decisions, especially as a man's ability to support his children never was a Patriarchal consideration. Instead of doing his will, he instead did Thuthu's will, who in turn, did the will of the Matriarch.

Both Ani, and Thuthu entered a sexual relationship under conditions of Patriarchal law, and Matriarchal law, respectively, yet applied Matriarchal rules to the relationship, and then entered the Benign collective for judgment where Patriarchal rules applied to Ani.

THE LOWER SELF

The lower self is an energy field around the chest of men, and the heads of women. As can be seen when looking at the Patriarch's lower self above Osiris' head, the lower self consisted of a row of forty two minor serpents, figure 36. Depending on which collective a spirit incarnated from, a person had between eight, and twenty eight minor serpents in the lower self. [Osiris was a great spirit who incarnated at the sixth level of consciousness. The highest collective on earth began incarnating in 1974, and currently incarnates at the fourth level of consciousness.]

As can be seen, each minor serpent balances what seems to be a tiny 'crystal ball' above its head, figure 37. Inside each crystal ball, a tiny melodrama relating to a past life experience that changed the course of that lifetime continuously replays itself. For example, were Ani given a next lifetime, one drama in one crystal ball that would have been inserted above the head of a serpent in his lower self would have related to the flogging he allowed himself to receive under the auspices of the Matriarchal order, possibly from Thuthu herself. The words spoken by a man who overlaid him during the ordeal, would hae been repeated again and again to the ear of his spirit. Should he again have married, he would either not have had sex with his wife, or he would have married a woman below him in status.

Each tiny melodrama thus inserted, influences decisions

taken in subsequent lives. People and experiences sought out during a lifetime, can sometimes be explained in terms of past life experience. For this reason, abuse by a loved one in one life time, may lead to a choice of marriage partner for whom no love is felt, in a next lifetime, and so on.

Each minor serpent relates to an energy centre, or vital organ in the body, and each energy centre relates to relationships with others, or self. For example, the uterus relates to the mother, testicles relate to masculinity, breasts relate to the husband, the bladder relates to intimate relationships, the heart relates to the intimate partner, and so on. For this reason, energy centres can become afflicted when dramas contained within serpents in the lower self are activated by a person creating similar conditions in his or her current lifetime to conditions that disadvantaged them in a past lifetime.

The whole of life is about evolving the spirit in consciousness. For this reason, decisions previously taken are again taken, until the reasons they ended in failure in past lives can be resolved. Resolved issues lose their ability to negatively effect life outcomes, and physical health, while unresolved issues remain potential pitfalls.

Anxiety over planned actions often result from karmic memory. For example, any change induces a measure of stress. However, when a person wants to change his or her life by doing what in a past life led to negative outcomes, the stress produced by the mere intention to change is heaped on the stress produced in the psyche by the knowledge about what happened in a past life when a similar course of action was undertaken. For example, a woman who left a man in a past lifetime when job opportunities for women were scarce, and when divorce was socially frowned on, and who may have spiralled into lamentable circumstances of poverty, or lived with rejecting family, may experience extreme fear when divorce is again contemplated.

Should the woman who experienced such an outcome in a past life move for separation in a current lifetime, fear and anxiety relating to memory of what happened in a past life when the same course of action was taken, is likely to ensue. Should she move ahead in spite of the stress produced by the subconscious memory of what happened in a past life, body chemicals may induce symptoms in one or more organs related to marriage partnerships.

Should the woman undergo medical treatment for any symptoms she may experience, and therapy for the fear, job security should resolve inner conflict produced by fear of poverty, hardship, scandal, and loss of status.

The resolution of the fear induced by the memory contained within the crystal ball, results in healing of the energy centre attached to the minor serpent, and physical immunity to the disease the intention to change brought about. This acquired immunity is inscribed on the body's genes over twenty five years, and that immunity is imposed on the body the woman's spirit will inhabit during its next lifetime. In this way (winning in a present life where one lost in a past life), rewards that are everlasting are gleaned from experience hard bought.

Reincarnation differs from incarnation. People who live karmic lives feel that their lives are about something, but they do not know what. This feeling usually comes to a head after age twenty eight. Reincarnation firstly results from a spirit being blocked from resolving karma by another spirit who consistently incarnates with him, or her. Reincarnation secondly refers to the spirit again incarnating with the same soul, with other spirits it had lived with before, and in the same geographical area. This happens when there is karma owing to one or other individual by others. This ensures all involved run into a central crisis brought about by the same circumstances that resulted in the reincarnated spirit being owed karma, due to past life injustices against the reincarnated spirit. To ensure karma is balanced, a great spirit sometimes directly channels key individuals involved, driving each individual towards one central choice that results in karma being balanced. Hereafter, life either has no meaning to them at all, or life begins anew. Many who experience karmic lives have many experiences of deja vu, and some feel as if their actions are externally driven. [The film 'Reservoir Dogs,' is a film about reincarnation, although it might not have been intended as such by either the author of the story, or the producer of the film.]

A spirit is given seven lifetimes to balance karma relating to any single past lifetime. When karma is owing one spirit by others, the seventh lifetime can be given for no reason save to balance karma. When a spirit fails to clear karma through living a life of stagnation, obeying rules, and doing the will of others, the spirit loses the right to incarnate during ages of Division.

THE HIGHER SELF

A spirit house relates to an evolutionary growth path through which spirits it incarnates grow in consciousness. The growth path relates to growing a central character predisposition, or a central ability, see 'How Spirits Relate to the Collective,' below.

All people do not grow in the same way. Some grow through overcoming obstacles to physical health, some through overcoming psychological obstacles to success, some through raising large families, some through squandering inheritance, and so on.

The higher self, situated from about fifty centimetres above the head, contains a spirit entity called 'the house of spirits,' figure 14. Surrounding the house of spirits are twelve energy leafs that symbolically assume the form of twelve major serpents. Each serpent is given the house of spirits by an energy deity representative of one or the other house of astrology. [Each house of astrology is represented by an energy deity, such as the four lined up on the lotus before Osiris, figure 38.]

The serpents in the house of spirits relate to the fate the spirit house imposes on those it allows to incarnate under given sets of astrological variables. Each serpent in the house of spirits delivers an oracle pertaining to specific life outcomes to the house of spirits, figure 23.

While preparing Thuthu's spirit for incarnation as seven Patriarchal evil eyes, Osiris' higher mind was in contact with the house of the Patriarch. [The house of the Patriarch was primarily symbolised by the falcon, figure 39. By contrast, Osiris' house was symbolically represented by Ani's bird-man house of spirits.']

Major karma is karma that relates to injustices against self, while minor karma relates to injustices against others. Major karma is placed in the house of spirits, minor karma is placed in the lower self, while injustices by others against the spirit during its lifetimes are recorded in the higher mind. Destiny relates to the karmic contract the spirit entered with its spirit house at the beginning of the age during which the spirit began incarnating, see 'How to Make Yourself a Man.'

A spirit that does not do its will becomes increasingly feminine in appearance. A spirit who does what it 'feels' is wrong becomes increasingly diffuse in appearance. Spirits who do their own will become increasingly masculine in appearance, while spirits who only do what they know is right become increasingly defined in appearance, as both Ani, and Thuthu indeed, were. Ani and Thuthu thus did what they believed was right, even if they did not do their will, but the will of the Matriarch. For this reason, their spirits appeared relatively effeminate, yet well defined. [Many times people learn to buy into belief systems they do not question, but accept the validity of. Such people often do what they think is right when even a moment's thought would convince them that they in fact do what others expect of them.]

On the lotus before Osiris four energy deities were aligned, figure 38. Each deity represented a house of astrology, and each deity pronounced an 'oracle,' or 'blessing' over each spirit leaf as it passed by. Each 'oracle' amounted to an energy leaf flying from each deity to the higher self of each spirit leaf. Each energy 'blessing' bestowed on the spirit thus lodged in the house of spirits of each spirit leaf that passed by the lotus.

Each major serpent in the higher self is thus nothing but a tiny spirit leaf, delivering a suggestion pertaining to one or the other life direction to the house of spirits. The fate their oracles, blessings, or psychic messages mediated in the lives of the men Thuthu's spirit would become, related to the four things that were important in a person's life at the first level of consciousness: self expression, work, family, and parents, and all are contained within the first four houses of astrology. [Surgical childbirth often results in the astrology being different to the astrology the spirit agreed to prior to incarnating. In this case, the spirit is recalled, and the person is a so-called 'soul-person' to whom astrology does not apply, as astrology applies to the spirit alone.

The first deity in front of Osiris on the lotus is the deity of the house of the rising sun. The house of the rising sun is represented by the first house of the astrological chart, and determines self expression. This deity had a detached goatee, figure 38.

The goatee symbolically was on the chin of male spirits at the fifth level of evolution, but not female spirits. The goatee represents the ability given a male spirit to impose an image previously imposed on him, on another person. Only at the sixth level of consciousness is a spirit able to use this ability for the benefit of others, and his own. The detached goatee meant that the men Thuthu's spirit would have became, would not have been able to impose the evil eye given them, on others.

The second deity, representative of the second house of astrology, determines life outcomes. The appearance of this deity indicates that each of the men Thuthu's spirit leafs would have become, would never have lived again at the level of consciousness Ani's and Thuthu's spirits had previously incarnated at.

The third deity determines family relations. This deity was black. Black is the colour associated with energy absorption, and entropy. The spirits would thus neither have been supported, nor would they have supported others in their social context.

The fourth deity determines relationships with the divine. The countenance of this deity means that there would have been no intervention in the lives of the men Thuthu's spirit would have become.

While energy from Ani's lower self flowed from Ani to rise in the stack before Osiris, psychic energy from the house of Horus, the house of family relations, flowed through Osiris' white helmet, down the black energy conducting chords on the side of his face, into his 'goatee,' to the four energy deities before him. They, in turn, imposed the energy they received from Osiris, and the energy they were given by the respective houses of astrology they represented, on the spirit leafs rising in the stack beside them. Over and above the psychic energy received from the house of the Patriarch, evil eyes from the house of the Patriarch moved down Osiris' person towards his feet, to the bottom of the lotus, to be imposed on the spirit leafs as they passed through. This evil eye pertained to Patriarchal values.

This means that the men Thuthu's spirit would have become, would have incarnated already inclined towards Patriarchal values. Although this evil eye was imposed on the men Thuthu's spirit would have become however, they were not in turn given the ability to impose the evil eye they received on others, the symbolic meaning of the detached goatee.

Ani and Thuthu would thus never again incarnate from the house of Osiris. Instead, Thuthu's spirit would incarnate as evil eyes from the house of the Patriarch, while Ani would never again incarnate.

UNDERSTANDING INCARNATION

Following a lifetime, the outer [oldest] layer of a spirit's energy, in other words, the layer with which the completed lifetime was started, is given the house of spirits as payment for the lifetime lived. One leaf is given the house of God for the services of the house of spirits. During ages of Benign Intervention, Patriarchy, and Matriarchy, one leaf was halved. One half layer was attached to the spirit as a right soul, the other was given the house of the alter ego. The left soul [genetically determined,] was sacrificed in case of alter ego overlay by an envious, or abusive parent born from the collective of the Alter Ego, a collective that does not incarnate during ages of Division. During ages of Division the left soul is joined by the spirit after age nine, and place is made for the arrival of the twin spirit after age forty five, the age of 'rebirth,' see 'Understanding Revelations.' The spirit leaf generated immediately before death is selected to begin the next lifetime.

Over and above the leafs given out as payment for each lifetime, and depending on the number of energy layers the spirit managed to grow during its lifetime, the spirit collects 'nest eggs' it keeps in reserve in the spirit house, figure 40. These nest eggs the spirit ingests at the end of a growth cycle before moving to a next, higher level of consciousness. The energy gives the spirit the density it requires to move to the next, higher level of consciousness his or her collective incarnates at, at the start of a new age.

Should a spirit be given an independent life as a new spirit house following a life of outstanding achievement, the so-called nest eggs that spirit accumulated during its lifetimes are incarnated on that spirit's behalf, as independent individuals. They return to the spirit at the end of their lifetimes, each bringing energy leafs they in turn worked to accumulate.

During the first three days of life, the spirit attaches loosely to the back of the infant, prepared to return to the collective, should it become apparent that the lifetime will not turn as expected. Sometimes people fall inexplicably ill for a day during early puberty, or once, or twice again, after. This happens when the spirit enters the body, attaching at the naval, behind the soul, leaf by leaf, figure 31. As the left soul is genetically determined, all people are thus soul people before their spirits enter their bodies. The soul's energy pulsates outward from the body to the rhythm of the spirit's heartbeat.

The last leaf built in any lifetime is the leaf with which a next life is begun, as I already mentioned. Because it was the last leaf built, it usually contains memory of events that led to death in the past life. Inexplicable fears of heights, torture, capture, prosecution, imprisonment, and so on, sometimes have their origin in a past life, especially if the fear experienced relates to an event that caused death. Usually, however, a spirit will yield no information relating to past life experience, as the spirit drinks from the proverbial 'river of silence' prior to incarnation. This is a symbolic ritual preceding incarnation, during which a spirit is not left without memory, but indeed enters a contract of silence with the universe.

During ages of Benign Intervention, Patriarchy, and Matriarchy, no leafs are generated after age fifty, unless life continues to be dynamic, changing, and supportive of the spirit's growth in consciousness. During ages of Division, no spirit ages beyond the age of forty five, as the spirit enters the fifth level of consciousness at that age due to the twin spirit joining forces with the original spirit to lead the individual to his, or her spirit mate, and his, or her highest calling. This requires the intervention of a great Spirit in the individual's life, and this in turn, follows a lifetime of outstanding dedication to uncovering the cause of self.

During a person's lifetime, energy layers grow from within the body, outward, almost as the year rings of trees grow from the core, outward. The density and amplitude of each new layer of spirit energy is influenced by the quality of food ingested, and life experience. The body gives the spirit energy during times of stress, resulting in low levels of physical energy.

Each new layer of energy is of a unique energy quality, as diet, emotional factors, and the extent of a person's involvement with his or her work, changes with time. The quality of the last layer of energy formed is extremely important, as it usually is the leaf with which the next lifetime is started. The importance of a person's involvement with issues of self development to the last second of life can thus not be overemphasized, as the conscious mind does not know when the spirit will stop building energy layers.

If diet is maintained, and if studious activities are pursued, many layers of quality energy can be formed during independent maturity. The more dense the layers of energy a spirit builds over a lifetime, the higher an individual's spirit density, and the more expensive the individual appears.

A person born from the house of the alter ego [now in the process of being discontinued,] began any lifetime with only one layer of spirit energy about one half an inch thick, undefined in shape, but not in consciousness, much as the leafs of Thuthu's energy appear, figure 19. At the fourth level of consciousness, where life is started with four layers of energy, the spirit still appears relatively diffuse, and undefined at the beginning of life, although not as diffuse as the single layer with which life at lower levels of consciousness is begun.

Towards the end of a lifetime however, the body's genes are inscribed on the spirit's energy, as a result of which the spirit begins to resemble the body in appearance. Compare, for example, how relatively transparent, diffuse, and undefined in appearance the single layers of Thuthu's spirit's energy behind Osiris appear, figure 19, compared to Thuthu's complete spirit, comprising several layers of the same spirit energy, figure 8. Clearly, Thuthu's fea tures were well-defined, distinctly human-like, and conveyed character, as she entered the Hall of Judgment. This is how energy density affects physical appearance. Still, Thuthu's astral body was less evolved than Ani's, as her spirit was white, while Ani's astral body assumed the colour of his skin during life, figure 10.

Life is expensively bought, and each lifetime is preceded by childhood experience that inevitably saddles each person with resentment, and psychological obstacles to overcome as best possible, before adulthood success can be aspired to. This is why a spirit will fight to maintain life against staggering odds for as long as it is able to believe that it will be able to achieve growth in spite of shorter term stagnation, or adversity. Sometimes the conscious mind pulls the spirit through, as the conscious mind sees chance to deal with evil no spirit will ever deal with. But sometimes the conscious mind overrides the will of the spirit, and does the will of others, or society. This results in the spirit withdrawing, and feelings of anxiety, and emptiness, ensuing.

KARMIC CONTRACTS
(Understanding Energy Transfer and Psychic Contracts)
The Concept of 'Curse'

The curse amounted to an energy insert in the so-called 'Underworld' into 'cursed' people's hands, feet, and gums that rendered others averse to them. Following the cursed life, energy inserts were again removed from the spirit, prior to the spirit again incarnating, figure 41.

The karmic 'curse' was symbolised by animal archetypes,

typically small animals of prey, rodents, cray fish, lizards, spiders, and snakes. These small life forms represented 'consciousness of misfortune' that was intuitively felt by others, and that rendered others averse to cursed persons.

Cursed persons were unlucky in specific ways, for example, in self expression, in agriculture, in handling glass, and so on. Cursed persons were not susceptible to infections or disease. However, they were carriers of disease, were often hyper sexual, and became compulsively, imposingly and prematurely intimate with strangers.

If such people touched others, either sexually, or violently, the energy 'curse' was transferred from their hands, and entered the energy fields of those they touched in circumstances of emotional arousal. In the end, genes contained within the 'energy curse' found their way from the energy fields of people who touched cursed persons into their bodies, the energy curse settling in body areas that symbolised faculties that related to the cursed person at the moment of energy transfer. For example, the colon is symbolic of self expression, the bladder is symbolic of anger, the head is symbolic of the spirit, the lungs are symbolic of the will to receive, and so on. In this way, persons who related to cursed persons under conditions of emotional arousal eventually contracted ailments, or tumours in body organs that related to cursed persons.

PSYCHIC CONTRACTS

The Matriarchal collective immediately came under Lucifer's auspices, after his arrival. At this point, Apep began working as an incarnating spirit in Europe until he joined the new Incarnating fraternity at the beginning of the previous century as an Incarnating spirit.

The difference between Satan and the Devil is that Satan is an energy entity who opposes the will of an individual to make himself more than he is allowed to be under Matriarchal law, as the story of Job illustrates. The devil on the other hand, waits until an individual arrives at a cross roads in his life. At this point, alternative courses of action are suggested. The choice made determines outcomes, and teaches the individual in question what they need to learn. Satan relates to the house of the Matriarch, while the devil works under the auspices of the God of Gods.

Although the Underworld no longer exists, it remains possible to receive spirit overlays from strangers, or family during times of emotional upheaval, and alter ego overlays from family members born from the collective of the alter ego during times of sexual excitement, or emotional upheaval.

Such spirit overlays are called 'psychic contracts' and they make it impossible for an individual to ever be what he or she potentially incarnated to become, in addition to their presence in the psyche resulting in ongoing feelings of anxiety. From this perspective, alter ego energy in the psyche may be thought of as 'Satan.' [Alter ego overlays can only be received from family members incarnated by the collective of the Alter Ego.]

Psychic contracts amount to intention-carrying energy leafs about one half an inch thick, and about the size of a saucer, being transferred from the energy field of one person into the energy field of another. Psychic contracts between parents and children were often unilateral in the past, yet accepted by past Incarnating fraternities, as parents' jurisdiction over children was absolute.

A psychic contract amounts to the parent deciding at the conscious level to use the child to advantage himself, or herself, in one way or the other. For example, a parent may assume that a child will support him, or her, after their retirement. For fear of the child rejecting this parental intention, the parent does not discuss his or her intention with the child. Instead, the most desired child receives an energy overlay from the parent's spirit, overlaying the child's higher mind. After a few years, the child begins thinking about allowing the parent to live with him, or her. [Parenting represents a major psychological challenge. Being a good parent does not come naturally to many people, and entering unilateral contracts with children, historically was part of parenting. The key here is to be honest about one's intentions with a child. Once evil intent is consciously noted, it disappears.]

Where children are sexually excited in the presence of parents born from the collective of the alter ego, children are most likely to receive alter ego overlays from parents whose sexual dreams remain unfulfilled. Where emotional arousal does not elicit inner conflict about sexual values, ego overlays may transfer from parents to children.

THE EGO OVERLAY

During times of emotional upheaval, relating to a parent's feelings of loss of self, a parent may deposit a leaf of spirit energy relating to his, or her innate talent on the higher mind of his or her child, should the parent think that the child could carry his or her talent to fruition. This amounts to the parent imposing his talent on the child. At the conscious level, the parent wants the child to achieve when the parent could not. At the subconscious level, the parent wants the child to achieve, in the child's life, what the parent was meant to achieve in his or her life. The subconscious intention represents evil intent on the part of the parent, as a spirit is judged on whether or not he did his own will, and his own assigned work. Here, the parent's energy lodges between the child's spirit, and his higher mind, actively blocking the child's conscious mind from ever knowing his own spirit's work.

A second case that often comes into existence relates to a child's will for himself becoming the parent's will for him. In this way, the child's will is taken from him. The reason is that the child feels as if he is doing the parent's will each time he does his will. Eventually, the child withdraws from doing his will in order to do his will. The conflict this induces brings freedom to the child from parental oppression, but ensures the child never succeeds at his assigned work, as the child then needs to find alternative avenues of self expression.

At this point, the attention of the Incarnating fraternity of Division is drawn to the child-parent relationship, and the parent's lot is assigned the child. This means that, upon the parent's death, the parent's spirit is destroyed, so that the parent stops existing as a separate entity. To protect the child against possible invasion by the parent's spirit following the parent's death, the child's collective is attached to the parent. It is thus important parents follow their own dreams, and assume supportive, yet unimposing roles in their children's lives.

During ages of Benign Intervention, Patriarchy, or Matriarchy by contrast, the parent's collective connected to the child's higher self, and the child was assigned karma because he 'allowed' the parent's energy overlay to attach to his energy field. Here, the child experienced interfering stimulus when doing any work. He felt distracted, and ran interfering 'thoughts.' This interference was the result of the parent's spirit leaf lodging in the child's higher mind, and connecting with the parent's collective. A kind of subconscious conversation that drew the child in, began whenever concentration was required. The result was an immediate drop in scholastic performance, anxiety, and the child physically appearing as if somehow threatened.

In cases where parents overlay a child to live through the child, the energy received from the parent is relatively dense due to age and experience, compared to the child's energy field, which is relatively diffuse. The younger the child, the more likely the parent's energy leaf will exert influence over the child's choices. As the child matures, the child is likely to feel increasingly drawn to the parent's field of interest, while the parent is likely to take a keen interest in the child's 'talent.' With time, the child is likely to carry the parent's talent to fruition, in the child's lifetime, and by the child's effort.

During ages of Patriarchy, Matriarchy, and Benign Intervention, the parent recalled his energy through the relevant spirit collective, following his, or her life. In this instance, the parent's energy was immediately collected from the child. The child's effort then accrued to the parent, who was given a subsequent lifetime as if he or she had fulfilled his or her contract with his, or her spirit house. The child's energy field was left with a gaping void, and the child's spirit was indicted upon its return to the collective for having failed in his, or her life mission.

Should the parent's energy have returned to the parent during the child's working life during ages of Patriarchy, Matriarchy, or Benign Intervention, the child would have been left with feelings of loss of interest in his work, contemplated career changes, or he would have sunk into depression, often for years, as the parent's energy leaf consumed the child's energy in the child's faculty of innate talent.

During ages of Benign Intervention, Patriarchy, and Matriarchy, energy transfer from one spirit to another was taken to imply that the receiving spirit accepted the will of the imposing spirit for it. In this way, the symbiotic relationship of energy transfer from one individual to another, often led to suffering for some individuals, wasted lifetimes for others, and unearned rewards for yet others.

During ages of Division, a spirit imposing its energy on another is given a month to find it. Unless it can retrieve what it imposed on another, it is destroyed, due to its having stolen another's life to advantage himself, or herself. Here, his or her talent is left with the spirit he or she imposed on.

THE ALTER EGO OVERLAY
(Thou Shalt Not Excel)

Should the parent's spirit want to stop the child achieving the child's potential altogether, in other words, should jealousy have the power to cause the parent to want to make the child less than he, or she potentially can be, an overlay from a parent born from the collective of the alter ego to the child's higher mind could overlay the child's seat of intellectual power by its shifting between the child's higher mind, and his, or her house of spirits, cutting him off from karma he is meant to heal through his life experience.

Alter ego energy entering a child's energy field carries the intention of the person who overlaid the child, for the child. This energy intention opposes the child's spirit in its desire to do its will, in addition to systematically swaying the child's spirit to do the will of the one who overlaid him, while simultaneously seeking to align others' spirits against the overlaid child's spirit.

In the worst cases of parental jealousy, the Alter Ego himself connects to the child's higher mind. Here, the child feels unable to 'get through' to the solution of a problem, question, or challenge. This results in intense, and ongoing anxiety, tense body posture, and the child waking up at night in terror. The injustice in this is beyond imagining.

Teenagers who behave sexually in parents' presence with opposite sex partners, may receive alter ego energy leafs containing information about the parents' unfulfilled sexual dreams overlaying their higher minds. [Even children who are particularly beautiful to alter ego parents, may suffer this fate.] The immediate

72

result of this kind of overlay is a sudden change in physical stature, changes in facial appearance, weight gain, drop in scholastic performance, and over-interest in opposite-sex relationships. Here, the child feels 'less' if he or she is not part of a sexual relationship.

In spite of their obsessive interest in relationships, such children never experience their sexuality as it was before they received the energy overlay. Once adults, such children may have smaller genitals than normal, and may be extremely worried about their relative sexual appeal to others. As soon as sexuality ensues, neutrality sets in, enjoyment fades, and interfering thoughts begin.

The most insidious effect of the alter ego overlay, as a direct result of physical punishment (demonstrated in the case of Ani), is that energy the soul should give the body, and spirit, is channelled from the soul to the alter ego collective. Feelings of fatigue, feelings of despondency, and lowered intelligence that can never be overcome, result.

Any energy overlay is a small leaf of spirit energy with consciousness. In fact, it effectively is a spirit 'person' with awareness, and intention. It attaches itself to the overlaid person's house of spirits. From here, it overpowers the house of spirits, and talks to the spirits of other people the overlaid person meets. In the so-called 'fifth dimension,' it tells others' spirits sensitive secrets about the individual it overlaid. This results in feelings of self consciousness in the overlaid individual, as others simply feel that there is just something they dislike about the overlaid person, or they pity the overlaid individual, leading to feelings of inferiority in the overlaid person. Worse yet, in heterosexual relationships the alter ego overlaid woman's overlay seeks to align her husband against her.

People who overlay, differ from those they overlay. The

73

overlaid individual is mentally superior to the overlaying person. The person who overlays is invariably unable to rise to where he or she believes they ought to be by their own effort. The overlaying individual holds the person they overlay in contempt. This means that they hold a negative image of a person who is superior to them, in their mind's eye. In the worst cases, they actively think scandalous, or down spiralling thoughts about the overlaid person, often in the overlaid person's presence. The effect of alter ego overlay is pleasing behaviour, and the overlaid person experiencing ambivalent emotions towards the individual who overlaid him, or her.

In the worst cases of alter ego overlay, the Alter Ego attaches to the overlaid individual. Connection with the Alter Ego can be immediately, externally observed, as it results in the body appearing as if it is consciously held upright. The chin seems somewhat thrust forward, the face 'looks up' at others, and the posture is mildly rigid. The person interrupts others in conversation, and has to learn to be attentive. This physical posture symbolically expresses the threat that the spirit experiences within. In the worst cases of Alter Ego connection, schizophrenia ensues. The Alter Ego underlies all mental, and psychosomatic disease.

Most often, resentment between parents and children result from karmic contracts coming into existence that both parties are only subconsciously aware of. The person at the receiving end of the contract invariably feels inexplicable feelings of resentment towards the one who overlaid them. Those who overlaid, on the other hand, feel inexplicable feelings of being above those they so overlaid, in spite of their being inferior.

Master-slave relationships have dominated human relation ships throughout the ages, as spirits were never able to enter the collective to be judged independently, but always needed to enter as either alter egos, souls, or ego partners in relation to other spirits. In this way, relatedness superceded growth considerations for all mankind's history.

This situation was brought to a halt at the turn of the last century, when Apep was given a chance by the incoming fraternity to apply the rules of Division in China, and Eastern Europe, while he did the same in the Western world. Immediately, female disempowerment made way for greater male-female equality, and the karmic image of the woman changed.

Strengthening the spirit over the alter ego is achieved by a person focussing on doing his or her assigned work, living by ego values, and moving away from individuals towards whom ambivalent feelings are felt. Doing the will of self never amounts to reactive behaviour. Reactive behaviour belongs to the alter ego spirit. The ego goes about its business without imposing itself on others, and without disadvantaging others.

THE HAND SHAKE

When people shake hands, their spirits speak to one another in the fifth (spirit) dimension. To better understand agreements reached during hand shakes, let us imagine that a woman wished to sell her property, and that a potential buyer arrived to view her property with an agent.

At the moment of his arrival at her apartment, the potential buyer extended his hand in a gesture of self introduction. His conscious mind wanted to buy a better property than he had, but his spirit, for one reason or the other, did not. Spirits sometimes have agendas that conscious minds know nothing about, and go about exerting a powerful influence on the outcome of events in the way described here.

At the objective level, the potential buyer felt confident. Upon shaking the seller's hand however, the two spirits entered into an agreement that the seller would not sell her property to the potential buyer. At the conscious level, neither had knowledge of this agreement. Both, however, were aware that their hand shake had lasted a second too long.

While the agent escorted the buyer through, the seller uncharacteristically sat down at her desk, leaving the sale to the estate agent, who also felt surprised that the hand shake had lasted for what seemed an extended time. At the end of the viewing, the buyer wanted to know whether the apartment was very sunny, as he was worried that the apartment would be cold in winter. The seller felt inexplicably nervous that the buyer did not want a very sunny apartment. She untruthfully answered that the apartment did not get that much sun.

When the buyer left, the seller consciously felt a vague feeling of hollow discomfort, as if she had done what she had not consciously wanted to do. When the buyer offered on her property, felt inexplicable feelings of resistance to selling the property, and declined the offer.

Was her spirit sabotaging her?

Dragging feet often relates to a spirit having reasons for not wanting to pursue a course of action against knowledge it has, that the conscious mind does not have.

The seller still lives in her apartment, thinking what a fool she would have been, had she sold a comfortable riverside apartment she would not have been able to afford to replace.

As consciousness increases, both men and women acquire better conscious understanding of which outcomes they want to effect. At higher levels of consciousness the female experience becomes more difficult, as the inclination to do the will of self becomes more powerful with age. Men too, at this level of consciousness experience needs for having things their way. For lack of authority, they sometimes dominate their domestic world, of which their sexual relationships, and their wives [already looking for greater autonomy,] are part. Women, at this level of consciousness, begin to find husbands' efforts at steering their relationships towards an apparently preconceived end, hurtful, if not threatening. In addition, some older husbands' needs to impose their need for sexuality on women they emotionally abused during youthful immaturity must account for the majority of divorces in later years.

Life is expensively bought, and each incarnation is preceded by childhood experience that inevitably saddles a person with resentment, and psychological obstacles to overcome as best possible before adulthood success can be aspired to. For most people, no layers of energy are built after age fifty, the age at which most spirits begin consuming physical energy, leaving the body feeling weak, and tired. The importance of living a dynamic adult life of change, and growth until the last minute of life, from the spirit's point of view, cannot be overemphasized.

Although the spirit begins life as a single layer of energy at lower levels of consciousness, two layers at the second level, and four layers at the fourth level, the genes inscribed on the spirit nevertheless profoundly influence the genes of the body it inhabits. Physical evolution is slowed by this process, as spirit genes that evolved in previous eras are inscribed on modern physical genes. On the other hand, expensively bought consciousness, wisdom, and experience are preserved, and carried over from lifetime to lifetime by an incarnating spirit. In this way, a spirit's consciousness is escalated lifetime after lifetime.

The spirit grows through the stages of consciousness development his or her collective incarnates at, for one single age before beginning a new cycle of incarnation at a next level of consciousness, or being refused permission to incarnate at all.

The masculine spirit [whether expressing a male lifetime, or a female lifetime], leans towards doing its own will by doing its assigned work. The effeminate spirit leans towards supporting others' attempts at getting ahead, often at the cost of its own growth. The unevolved spirit leans towards doing the will of others, while the staid spirit leans towards imposing beliefs previously imposed on it, on others. When a spirit supports the growth of another spirit, while sacrificing its own growth [the growth of the other spirit being its reward,] that spirit is called a soul. Following life, this type of spirit returns to the house of souls; a great loss of status for a spirit.

The shift from one age to another takes about three hundred years to complete. Towards the end of each age, each spirit house incarnates as many spirits as possible. This enables it to collect as many 'modern' genes as possible back into itself before either being allowed to keep on incarnating itself, or being forced to discontinue incarnating.

At the end of each age, the universe removes each collective deemed unsuitable for life under the new paradigm. In this way, the face of the human experience changes during the first decades of each new age. Aquarius is the beginning of a golden age, and the beginning of a new brain structure evolving beside the old brain structure at first, which will pave the way for the spirit within to be joined by a partner-spirit later in life. This relationship within will in turn pave the way for a new male-female relationship without: the so-called spirit-mate relationship.

As Pisces began exiting in the 1950's, the new Incarnating fraternity introduced social change through the collective to which each person's higher self connects. The collective 'whispers' to the subconscious minds of all those who belong to it, which turn the tide is about to take.

At the beginning of Aquarius, the spirit collectives began telling spirits that authoritarian norms were no longer acceptable. Musicians like Buddy Holly, Elvis, and others, expressed unprecedented images of self that masses of people were ready to emulate. By the time those incarnated from 1955 had reached puberty, they felt intuitively drawn to opposite sex company, and felt comfortable accepting opposite sex peers as equals in the work place. This brought about a massive consciousness revolution during the 1970's that changed the face of Western society, and the position of women in the workplace, forever.

Not all people incarnate at the same level of consciousness, and no woman is below a man incarnated from a lower level of consciousness than she, simply because he is a man. Humans at the fourth level of consciousness have creativity, and relative understanding of the law of cause and effect. [During the age of Aquarius, the twin soul will be replaced by the twin spirit. Those who receive this gift will enter a new level of evolution, namely the fifth level of consciousness.]

Man is again entering a new evolutionary period, during which a new kind of sexual relationship will emerge. That relationship will commence after age forty, and will revolve around two people discovering their inner potential through their sexual relationship with each other. For the first time in man's history, every man and woman is able to live by the sweat of their brows and masculinize their spirits over what they were when their lifetimes began.

OTHER ARCHETYPES

During the creation spoken about in Genesis 2, a beast of prey was created to symbolise each negative survival trait. As people evolved, there inevitably came a time when every single incarnating spirit had overcome a specific survival trait, due to karma having been applied, lifetime after lifetime, for its expression. At that point, the animal that symbolised that specific survival trait became extinct. Only twenty eight species remain, mainly because of man's conservation efforts over the past sixty years.

Animals that symbolised negative survival skills, or traits, were called 'spirit animals.' For each negative survival trait symbolised by animal behaviour, there was a deity who judged the relative absence, or presence of that trait in a spirit in the Hall of Justice, or 'Hall of the Negative Confession,' figure 42. The will to live off another's efforts was deemed the most loathsome trait that ensured the survival of the morally lowest.

The hyena symbolised the Matriarchal sisterhood that excluded and disempowered males of their own kind [except when needed for conception.] This ensures the physical superiority of female animals at the cost of males who never learn to hunt, and who need mostly to scavenge.

The domestic cat's eyes, which differs from the eyes of large animals of prey, such as the lion, is an eye that symbolises a reptilian nature. Here, sexuality is driven by the singular desire to procreate to the exclusion of pleasure. Males routinely impose their sexuality on females, especially juvenile females who are prematurely, and sadistically raped in response to which they prematurely conceive. [Legend has it that a race of amber men with feline eyes once arrived on earth. They numbered two hundred thousand, and each one isolated, and raped a woman until she was pregnant. They had one large testicle, and each woman produced two infants: one male, and one female. The males' skins were amber, and they had brown eyes, while the females were White, with blonde hair and blue eyes. After twelve years on earth, they left with the male children, never to return.]

The wild dog entrusts parenting to weaker members of the pack. As a result, the pups are overlaid with 'weak' energy. The whole species is thereby weakened, generation after generation.

The chimpanzee female indiscriminately has sex with males when in season, to avoid being assaulted as a result of her turning down male sexual advance. Contrary to popular belief, she conceives with the weakest male, and not the strongest. In this way, bullies are eliminated from the gene pool, and safety for offspring is enhanced. On the other hand, physical strength is sacrificed, especially in female offspring.

At higher levels of consciousness, negative survival strategies amount to weaknesses that render a person offensive to others, but at lower levels of consciousness, offensive strategies often win.

FACES OF AGES

Like a body carries genes in its cells, a spirit carries genes inscribed on its energy field. At the first level of consciousness spirits appear as crosses. At the second level of evolution they appear ss clay tablets, hence the traditional appearance of tomb stones. At the third level, they are undefined, almost as the ghosts portrayed as Caper's brothers in the comic series 'Casper, the Friendly Ghost.' At the fourth level of consciousness they begin to appear as humans, but are relatively transparent, and diffuse.

At the lowest levels of consciousness evolution Matriarchy represents a system of escalating genetic weakness by eliminating the strong through sacrifice. Invariably, the Matriarch incarnated a person who was a proverbial 'keeper of contracts' into each primitive society. This kind of spirit was symbolised by the dog, figure 6. The 'dog spirit' usually was a medicine man of sorts. His subconscious mind alerted the Matriarchal collective about goings on in the tribe. Often, the Matriarchal collective channelled the dog spirit as to which course of action to take against those who opposed Matriarchal principles. At this time, the witch doctor, or medicine man got the feeling that someone needed to be sacrificed. [Legend has it that Chaka Zulu was murdered shortly after he saw through witch doctors' agenda with tribal seances during which supposed 'thieves' would be pointed out, and stabbed on the spot, before anyone could intervene.] At higher levels of consciousness, Matriarchy sacrifices the strong to the support of the weak.

Past Matriarchal ages witnessed atrocities committed against children. Female children born to women without husbands were routinely sold as sex slaves as early as age five, and were hideously 'trained' by Matriarchal men, and women in so-called 'temples,' and brothels. Children who resisted genital, or anal manipulation were routinely head butted, so that mental retardation, emotional withdrawal, and schizophrenia were common. Male children were no better off than females. Those who were caught masturbating, or having sex with other slaves during night time were castrated, and iron hooks were burned into their arms so that they could be locked to stakes.

The tenets of Patriarchy are well represented by Islam. Patriarchy is about eclipsing the female principle. Since the age of Taurus, female collectives in Patriarchal societies have incarnated under Matriarchal auspices, while the male collectives remained under the auspices of the Patriarch. In Patriarchal societies, men are thus born from the house of the Patriarch, while women either incarnate from the house of the Matriarch, or from the house of the Patriarch. [Male spirits incarnate as women for reasons of violating Patriarchal male-female value-transfers during their lifetimes.]

In Patriarchal societies, Matriarchy thus represents a system of female disempowerment of women by women. In return for physical support and security, women sacrifice self fulfilment, self expression, and doing their own will, a survival strategy symbolised by the domestic dog. In Matriarchal societies however, Matriarchy represents a system of human disempowerment as a result of the Matriarch's supposed need to avenge the wrongs committed against women in Patriarchal societies.

Between about 30BC and 500AD, conflict arose between

the Creator and the Patriarch, who liaised with Lucifer against the Creator's strategy to resurrect women *and* men who had abstained from sex throughout their lives. He thus had the same entry criteria for men and women. [He was at any rate convinced that people should sacrifice sex by only having sex when conception was desired. He argued that, once people had children they could not support, they could not apply themselves to ongoing tuition, or change whenever growth demanded it.]

In the modern context, sacrifice of sex need not be contemplated. To sacrifice sexuality is to sacrifice the life force within. Moreover, the process of personal growth can only begin after age forty five, when life experience enables understanding of matters of the spirit. By this time, children produced during youthful inexperience have achieved independency, thus setting parents free to choose new directions, or not.

Following his fall, the two hundred women who served in temples at Heliopolis [the reason for the Creator's conflict with Lucifer and the Patriarch], were sold to the Patriarchs, resident in Libya since their expulsion from Eden during the age of Taurus.

The women who were unwilling to have sex with the Patriarchs were sexually mutilated on pyres before being set alight. After one year, and more than one hundred sacrifices, the remaining women were rescued by the Matriarch's foot soldiers, who fled with them across the Alps into Italy under the leadership of the Matriarch, Garibaldi, an Italian by birth. The foot soldiers (who were Black men with long hair), were persecuted by the Patriarchs into Italy. Using the Matriarch's resources, the Patriarchs hunted them to near extinction. Those foot soldiers left over in Africa managed to escape in a boat, thereby avoiding genital mutilation, and crucifixion.

Enabling those evolved enough to move from the third, to the fourth level of consciousness was the reason Christianity was given man. Following the Patriarch's departure from Italy, Jehovah took the opportunity to introduce Christianity into Italy himself, setting himself up as the head of the Christian movement in place of the Creator. He reinterpreted Christianity, and destroyed most of the writings.

Having been sidelined yet again, the Patriarch formalised Patriarchal principles into what became known as the Koran, specifically to oppose Christianity, now presided over by Jehovah, and Hassim, opponent of the Patriarch. As a result of both Jehovah's and Hassim's participation, the principles of Benign Intervention found their way into Western collectives.

Following Matriarchal invasion of Heliopolis, the 'Holy Spirit' channelled the highest Incarnating spirit in the Universe about matters on the planet. In response, a new Incarnating fraternity began channelling information to selected people via the Holy Spirit. They eventually arrived one hundred years ago, having spent three hundred years looking for the planet which did not have 'a man (spirit) who speaks.'

A planet without a man (spirit) who speaks, may not be approached without being destroyed, as each planet receives a man who speaks at the beginning of time. All the time, while searching for the planet, they channelled technological information to the Holy Spirit, who in turn channelled ideas through to selected individuals. This brought about the first rudiments of technology, and Industry from the end of the seventeenth century. This would eventually set man free from family relationships that ensured survival, thus enabling man to begin focussing on growth in consciousness.

85

The paradigm of Benign Intervention was abruptly replaced by Division when the new Incarnating fraternity moved in to manage the Western, and Eastern collectives at the turn of the previous century. Western collectives, Eastern European collectives, and Japanese and Chinese collectives have been managed plus minus according to the rules of Division for the past one hundred years. At the same time, collective worship began falling into disfavour in the West, while disintegrating altogether in the East.

When consciousness is well evolved, so that individual behaviour need not be monitored by authoritarian rules, Division becomes possible. At this point, every man's psyche is able to receive a second spirit whose purpose is to join the first spirit in a work partnership that inaugurates a process called 'rebirth.' This state of consciousness was brought about over a period of only one thousand years by a new Incarnating fraternity that finally arrived at the turn of the last century to replace Jehovah's fraternity.

CHAPTER 2
THE STORY OF CREATION

The traditional assumption was that God created a flawless man, and placed him in an environment in which he could live without effort. Using part of this man's body, God made a woman to relieve his loneliness. This influenced man's perception of male-female relations, and left him idolizing a life of leisure.

Genesis 1 states from verse 26, 'Let us make man in our image, after our likeness: and let them have dominion ... So God created man in his own image, male and female created he them.'

Four things are important. Firstly, the God spoken about in Genesis 1, and Genesis 2, was the God of creation who allowed the Patriarch, who was the head of a group of forty spirit people, to create life in this solar system. The Patriarchs' descendants were mainly the Libyans, the Turks, and the Arabian people.

Secondly, there exists no discrepancy in time between the creation of male and female. Traditional religious interpreters misrepresented this fact, and attempted to portray the female as a later invention, created for the sake of the human male, in addition to emphasizing the Creator and other spiritual entities' maleness. This undoubtedly has left women feeling more removed from the Creator than those who supposedly belonged to his sex.

Thirdly, man and woman are in their image. This suggests that the group of which the Creator was part consisted of males and females. Fourthly, 'them' refers to man plus woman, 'male and female created he them' (Genesis 1:27). In Genesis 1:28 God blessed them, and gave them dominion over creation. The explicit intention at the outset was thus that men and women should share dominion over creation, as they now do. This is an important consideration, as things historically did not pan out according to this early intention. Instead, men grabbed power, exalting themselves to the status of 'man,' as opposed to 'woman,' when these two terms respectively referred to the spirit, and the soul, within, and when all is said and done, not all men receive spirits, and not all women are soul people.

Moving now to Genesis 2, the reader need remind himself, or herself that the traditional assumption was that Genesis 2 represented an explanatory account of Genesis 1. The reader will ascertain for himself, or herself, that the text does not support this assumption.

The creation spoken about in Genesis 1, began about three hundred thousand years ago, and ended about one hundred and fifty thousand years ago. By contrast, the creation spoken about

in Genesis 2, began about thirty thousand years ago, it represented a recreation of what went before, and it followed planetary devastation brought about by the removal of the earth's
atmosphere. The restructuring of the creation spoken about in
Genesis 1 ensued during the previous age of Aquarius, approximately twenty six thousand years ago.

This recreation followed the removal of earth's atmosphere
to reduce Matriarchal numbers, and eliminate all the people and
animals the Matriarchs had created. Adam left the garden of Eden
more than twenty thousand years later.

In support of the fact that Genesis 1 and Genesis 2 represent
relations about different creations, Genesis 2 begins by telling the
reader that, at some point after the seventh day, the Creator
reassessed the earth situation, 'And every plant of the field before it
was in the earth, and every herb of the field before it grew.'

The question that springs to mind is, before what? The
answer is: before 'something' caused the field to stop growing as
it had in Genesis 1:12, 'and the earth brought forth grass, and
herb.' Logically, only a cataclysm of sorts could stop the field
growing as it had.

The lifting of the planet's atmosphere had lasted for approximately one hundred and thirty years, after which the state of the
plants was described, firstly in terms of the fact that the plants grew
before 'it,' secondly, in terms of the fact that the plants and seeds
remained capable of growing, and thirdly, in terms of the fact that
this growing and germinating depended on rain falling, 'for the
Lord God had not caused it to rain upon the earth' (Genesis 2:5).

It is not logical to think that verse 5 could mean that a rain
cycle had not yet been created as Genesis 1:7, which relates events

preceding the seventh day, states that dividing 'the waters which were under the firmament from the waters which were above the firmament,' was one of the first things effected during the first creation epoch. In addition, Genesis 1:12 makes it abundantly clear that the plants created before the seventh day brought forth fruits and seeds, which means that water was indeed available. Moreover, verses 1 through 3 of Genesis 2 make it clear that the Creator retired from a job that worked as planned, 'Thus the heavens and the earth were finished,' and that he retired for the duration of a period which was called 'the seventh day.'

This means that the rain cycle originally created was interrupted by an event described in ancient language, the original translator could not find an appropriate translation for, as a result of which he substituted a term he could not understand by the word, 'it,' meaning 'something or the other.'

The fact that the rain cycle could again to be instated, lends further credence to the argument that the cataclysm that laid the creation spoken of in Genesis 1 low, could not have been a meteoritic collision. A meteorite burns the atmosphere as it enters, and destroys the spirit energy that overlays the earth, baking the soil in such a way that the rain cycle around the area of impact can never again be instated, and the soil can never again be arable, except when treated with chemicals that are manufactured once people reach an advanced stage of consciousness. That this in fact happened around Sodom and Gomorrah, is spoken about in Genesis 11.

The process whereby a rain cycle is created entails inducing fusion in a planet's core. This triggers a major volcanic eruption, which opens the way for the rest of the process to be introduced, simultaneously with induction of fusion. This can only be done thrice, provided there is hydrogen left in the core [of which there no longer is enough in the earth's core.] At the same time, a spirit entity envelopes the planet, causing the water vapour to be 'caught' in its energy. The appearance of this process from the planet's face is approximately described in Genesis 2:6, 'But there went up a mist from the earth, and watered the whole face of the ground.'

Appraising the situation after 'it' had occurred, the Creator thus observed that the plant-situation required a rain-cycle [again] be instated. More importantly, however, looking again, he perceived that there was not a man to till the soil.

Returning now to Genesis 1:28, after the creation of man, before the period of retirement [seventh day] and the subsequent cataclysm 'it,' it is clear that the Creator blessed the man [male and female] he had created, specifically intending them to 'Be fruitful and multiply, and replenish the earth, and subdue it.'

Multiplication would have come as it did to all animals. However, to subdue something is to overcome the resistance to your will it offers, and make it what you want it to be. To replenish the earth means to put back into the earth what was taken from it. Both actions presuppose effort, and, in the absence of technology, immense effort.

The point with man's creation from the beginning was thus to bring about a man that possessed traits that could motivate him to expend effort changing his environment. Traditional interpreters missed this intention, hence their postulation that man was created perfect, and that the Creator intended eventually to give man eternal life on a platter.

An animal will not expend effort unless it is firstly able to conceptualize the advantage to itself in such a course of action, and secondly, unless it desires that advantage. The mental traits of desire, and the ability to compare the existing to the ideal, are thus indispensable in such a creature. No entity innocent of desire will expend the kind of effort tilling soil demands.

In a second attempt at effecting this kind of man, the Patriarch and the Creator, 'formed man of the dust of the ground' (Genesis 2:7). [It is important the reader note the difference between the Creator, who was able to engineer life from matter, and the Patriarch, who was able to create life from genes already in existence.]

Although it may be reasonably argued that, since no plants had been around for one or the other period of time (Genesis 2:5), and since all animals, including man, were herbivorous (Genesis 1:29-30), there may possibly have been nothing left alive by the catastrophe that necessitated the Creator's readdressing the planetary situation. The text however rather suggests that life still existed, and that those existing life forms were restructured.

In further support of the argument that life still existed, but needed altering, possibly also in view of climatic changes following 'it,' the verb 'form' in Genesis 2 pertains to action in which something is reorganized by some kind of effort from one shape into another. It pertains to action that meliorates.

While 'forming' thus undoubtedly contains an element of creation, the reason the word 'form' was used in Genesis 2, while 'made' and 'created' were used in Genesis 1, would have been to set what happened in Genesis 2 apart from what happened in Genesis 1. That a new man emerged from a man already in existence, is evident from reading the wording of the text. Having 'formed' [meliorated] man, man became what he had, in other words, not been: a living [incarnating] spirit.

It seems reasonable to think that, in order for something to become one thing, it must first exist as another thing. For man to become a living soul, he had therefore to have first existed as something other than a living soul. This is also supported by the fact that animals were formed 'out of the ground' (Genesis 2:19). 'Dust,' on the other hand, pertains to ground that is raised from the crust body, in a state of suspension (mobility), and represents a more diffuse state of 'ground.' 'Forming' man, brought about Adam, a man who was set further apart from beasts than man had been, before.

That a melioration rather than a creation took place is further supported by the fact the Creator put the man he had formed in a garden he had planted. The text is phrased in such a way that it appears a relocation effected a separation of the formed man from others not so formed, 'God planted a garden eastward in Eden; and there he put the man whom he had formed' (Genesis 2:8). That he planted the garden is an obvious, and further indication that the plants needed to establish a garden already existed.

That Genesis 1 and 2 tell different stories about different creations is also supported by the fact that man was formed in Genesis 2 before the beast and fowl, while in Genesis 1 he was created, after. Moreover, Genesis 2:5 does not state that there was not a man. It states that there was not a man to till the ground.

Verses 10 through 14 convey a physical location of this garden, pointing to a location somewhere in Ethiopia, possibly adjoining Egypt. Eden and the garden however, were two different things. The story traditionally was told in such a way that they became confused as the same thing. It emerges from the text that Eden was an area within which the garden was established, 'God planted a garden eastward in Eden' (Genesis 2:8), and 'a river went out of Eden to water the garden' (Genesis 2:10).

In the whole story of Adam, the garden was never once called 'paradise,' and was never alluded to as a place of, or a state of perfect happiness. It was simply a place that was cultivated for the purpose of engineering a man capable of desiring to become more than he was at any given time.

Personal growth, or growth in consciousness, is closely linked to man's struggle for material gain. On the other hand, feelings of depression, anger, stress, and despondency result from a man working to support others, without simultaneously serving his spirit's growth purpose.

In verse 18, consistent with his stated intention to create a man who desires to have more, or to be more, the Creator observed room for improvement in Adam's make-up. He felt that something was yet amiss, 'It is not good that the man should be alone; I will make an help meet for him.'

'Make an help meet for him' could not ever have meant 'make a wife, woman, or partner for him.' This 'help' had to come in the form of something that could evoke the desire to have, in Adam. The aim here was not to evoke a desire for more sex in Adam, but to elicit a desire to have more at the material, aesthetic, and consciousness levels, 'the woman saw that the tree was good for food [material], and that it was pleasant to the eyes [aesthetics, or enjoyment], and a tree to be desired to make one wise [growth in consciousness,'] (Genesis 3:6).

That the purpose of the Creator specifically was to create a desire to change his world in Adam, and that the creation of a woman had nothing to do with what transpired, is supported by the fact that Adam was a collective noun pertaining to a kind of human, specifically the one into whom was blown the breath of life, 'Male and female created he them, and called their name Adam' (Genesis 5:2). In other words, Adam was a tribe of people who already consisted of males and females. Moreover, the Creator first tried to solve Adam's aloneness-problem by 'forming' animals and bringing them to Adam to name, 'I will make an help meet for him. And out of the ground the Lord God formed every beast, and brought them unto Adam to see' (Genesis 2:18-9). In other words, the Creator hoped to cure the aloneness-problem of the man by first meliorating the animals, and offering Adam ownership of them. This did not have the desired result. By verse 20, Adam had named all the animals, 'but for Adam there was not found an help meet for him.'

Adam's melioration thus still left him without the mental faculties that underlie desire, and therefore the motivation to engage effort to change his environment. Evidently, the fact that something referred to as 'the man' was alone, was the Creator's diagnosis as underlying Adam's lack of ambition. The rib intervention was thus intended to effect a response [to desire to have more, and to be more] that the animal-melioration had failed to elicit.

Since Adam thus already consisted of males and females, we may safely surmise that 'the man' to whom reference is made, was not the males among Adam. Similarly, 'the woman' in question emerged as a result of the Creator's second attempt at solving the problem [lack of ambition] brought about by the aloneness of 'the man,' and was thus likewise not a human female.

In summary, 'the man' refers to something within Adam: a mental faculty which, alone, left Adam unable to desire, even when invited to make something his own, and that faculty was the spirit. 'The woman,' on the other hand, was something that emerged as a result of one or the other intervention aimed at bringing about the trait of desire in man.

The soul was originally given to induce desire, and to provide the body with energy. The soul is the feminine part of the human psyche, and soul energy is taken from spirit energy. The leafing of Thuthu's spirit in Ani's story illustrates the process whereby a spirit found to be inclined to doing others' will, is 'reduced' to either alter egos, or evil eyes. Genetic altering nevertheless is an indispensable part of changing psychic arrangement, as changes in brain structure alone increases psychic complexity.

Spirits inclined to support other spirits' evolution at the cost of their own growth, are reduced to souls by the same 'leafing' process, although the 'programming' does not take place.

The rib intervention entailed genetic restructuring that enabled an additional psychic component to be added to the spirit, and this component was the soul. A soul is a leaf of spirit energy that is programmed to support the spirit, much as an evil eye is a leaf of spirit energy that is programmed to convey an ideological principle of sorts to others.

Placing 'the woman' [soul] beside 'the man' [spirit], in Adam, elicited the desire to have more in Adam. The spirit desires to do, while the soul desires more, and desire emerged in Adam shortly after 'the woman' became a separate faculty of their psychological make-up. The rib intervention thus cured the aloneness of 'the man' in Adam, not of Adam.

THE MEANING OF MARRIAGE

That the female aspect of self [soul], originally was part of the male aspect, that it was taken from the male aspect [spirit], and then added as a separate psychic component, following genetic alteration,   is supported by Genesis 2:23 'bone of my bones, and flesh of my flesh: she shall be called Woman [soul], because she was taken out of Man [spirit].'

The spirit was thus the 'man' spoken about in Genesis 2, while the soul was the 'woman.' Their relationship to one another rendered the man [spirit] the 'husband,' and the soul [woman, created to support the man in both women, and men.]

I already explained in the story of Ani and Thuthu, the relationship between soul and spirit within, is that the soul channels its energy to the spirit upon death. In other words, the soul becomes one with the spirit prior to death.   This relationship between soul and spirit within, was symbolised by the husband-wife relationship without.

The implication of oneness between man and woman relates to the fact that, following life, the wife's spirit was judged as the man's soul, 'Therefore [for the purpose of judgment] shall a man leave his father and his mother, and shall cleave unto his wife: and they shall be one flesh,' (Genesis 2:24).   The relationship between the spirit [man], and the soul [woman] within, was thus mirrored in the   husband-wife relationship without, 'as above, so below.' Here, the wife's spirit stops existing as a separate entity, and the woman's abilities accrue to her husband's spirit.

During ages of Division however, this principle falls away, and each spirit enters the collective alone. Souls [spirits who support others' growth at the cost of their own], are not again incarnated. Within the psyche, the soul is replaced by the twin spirit, or 'sister' spirit, after age forty five.   Following life, they bond to become what is known as a fraternal spirit, if both spirits belong to the earth collective.   The fraternal spirit then

97

moves on to incarnate at the level of consciousness associated with the onset of Division.

This represents the ending of the law given man at the beginning of time: that the man and woman will be one. In other words, the ending of the law represents the ending of the sacrifice of the female spirit to the evolution of the male spirit.

The 'sister' spirit is of the opposite sex to the spirit who originally incarnates. This ultimately balances the masculine, and feminine within. This balance is reflected in the physical spirit-mate relationship without. During ages of Division, each man or woman the universe chooses to work with receives an opposite sex spirit, in addition to the one they originally incarnated with, after age forty five. This is part of the process called 'rebirth,' and part of the process called the 'fulfilment [ending] of the law.'

During Benign Intervention, and Patriarchy, the spirit was not allowed to enter the collective without a wife [soul], who stood in for the man's [spirit's] transgressions. The purpose of marriage was thus to grow the male spirit at the cost of the female spirit, hence the ancient association between marriage and death. At the highest level of evolution, a spirit has its own growth as major objective, while supporting partners, and children in their respective needs to succeed.

Although the outcome of the rib intervention was thus traditionally interpreted as referring to the creation of a literal woman from the rib of a literal man, the text explicitly explains that 'the woman' was 'an help meet' that would not have been brought into existence, had the animal melioration succeeded in eliciting the desire to have more than he had, in Adam, a group of people which consisted of males and females, (Genesis 5:2.) The story about the woman being added to the man in Genesis 2, was thus a story about genetic intervention that changed the human psyche from a one-tiered system, to a two-tiered system, which then became a three-tiered system, following Adam's so-called 'fall from grace' some twenty thousand years later. This entailed further engineering which opened the soul to Alter Ego invasion, a hideous fate which opened man's spirit to collection by the Alter Ego since the age of Taurus.

CHAPTER 3
THE SNAKE, THE WOMAN, AND THE TREE OF KNOWLEDGE

It stands to reason that primitive languages' limited vocabulary would have combined with traditional translators' ignorance about man's psychological aspect, resulting in their having described all events as occurring at the physical level, their thus having mixed levels of abstraction. However, quite apart from the fact that primitive languages do not contain vocabulary with which to express psychological innuendoes, shame and embarrassment have to do with conscious awareness.

In spite of Genesis 2:25 stating that the man and his wife were naked and unashamed, this state of unashamedness [which came about during the age of Aquarius, some twenty five thousand years ago], was not a state of happiness, as it related to a state of innocence which did not relate to choice.

This condition was brought to an end by the intervention of the serpent, Apep, the archenemy of the Patriarch, and opponent of the Creator, during the most recent age of Taurus, figure 1.

Snakes do not speak to people, neither do they possess anatomical characteristics to enable such a fete. The serpent in the garden was not a literal snake at all, but a spirit collective whose collective character assumed the appearance of a serpent. The gold and black serpent was the alter ego collective during the age of Taurus, and Apep was the Incarnating spirit who presided over the collective.

The serpent was traditionally associated with healing, renewal, and eternal life. The reason was that serpents periodically shed their skins as a result of their growing in size, and in length. Climatic conditions influence the varieties of new patterns that emerge, following each shedding. During this time of change, they are vulnerable to enemies. So it is with the human spirit undergoing change, due to his or her having outgrown a previous image of self.

As everyone knows, man's so-called 'fall from grace' somehow became linked to his sexuality, although the exact connection between sex and Adam's 'fall' was not understood.

Having formed man from the dust of the ground, the woman's fertility remained tied to cycles of oestrus. Much as primates, human females conceived two-yearly. That human females did not conceive in past millennia as they now do, is supported by Genesis 3:16, which states, 'I will greatly multiply thy ... conception.'

Following the addition of the receptive soul to man's psyche twenty thousand years before, Apep became aware around six thousand years ago that the females among Adam were capable of sexual arousal in the presence of men, even when they were not in oestrus. In addition, Apep became concerned that the males among Adam were engaging in self stimulation, much as bored primates do. When females came into oestrus, competition among males ensued, as can be imagined. Women in oestrus were periodically raped by men they did not choose to have sex with, but who emerged victoriously from battles with other men. In short, human consciousness had evolved to a stage where sexuality needed to become linked to choice.

Hovering above the tree of knowledge was the spirit collective presided over by the spirit called Apep, figure 43. As one or more females gathered around to while away their day, they may suddenly have thought about approaching men of their choice for sex, in spite of their not being in season. It inexplicably, and suddenly may have occurred to the females that covering their genitals would make it impossible for men to tell whether or not they were in season, which would have circumvented the danger of men turning them down due to their not being physically receptive, or approaching them due to their being receptive. This would have enabled them to have sex by appointment, and with whom to have it when no one else was around. At the same time, they could turn down male advances when they were in season, by saying that they were not. [Alternatively, the women beneath the tree may have been approached by a man incarnated by the alter ego collective. He may have directly spoken to them, conveying such

103

previously unconsidered ideas to them.]

Be that as it might, conceptualizing the thought about cov-ering their genitals, approaching men for intercourse when not in oestrus, and actually having sex with men for reasons other than conception, constituted the woman 'eating from the tree of knowledge, and giving also unto her husband with her; and he did eat' (Genesis 3:6). This action by an instinct driven entity that clearly went against instinct, this receiving an idea from an external agent, constituted 'seeing' that the 'tree' was pleasant to behold, that it could potentially lead to increased wisdom, and that it was good for food [especially as the females soon demanded food in return for sex, which gave the men something to do, other than dominate one another.]

At this point, the Patriarch's attention was drawn to events in the garden. Upon his confronting the 'man,' that is, the spirit within the males and females among Adam, the spirit blamed the soul [woman] within, 'The woman whom thou gavest to be with me, she gave me of the tree' (Genesis 3:12).

An altercation between Apep and the Patriarch over the women's decision followed, after which the Patriarch invited the Matriarch to take over the female collective. At this point, Patriarchy, and Matriarchy amalgamated, figure 44. Matriarchal participation inaugurated an era of human misery in which slav-ery, child sex slavery, and injustice against both women and men, reached staggering proportions.

While 'the woman' and 'the man' within Adam in Genesis 2:25 were thus side by side, naked, and unashamed, by Genesis 3:6, this status had undergone change, so that a significant number of human males had become aware of their continuous need for sex, while females who were not in oestrus too, felt sexually aroused in some males' presence.

Following the women's subsequent experimentation with sex that related to choice, those who did not indulge at all soon were on the outside, looking in. Those who most indulged their sexuality soon had all the men about them, and food, dance, and song flowed to their huts. Soon, unpopular males formed bands, and raped women who lived with men they preferred. To protect themselves against sexual thuggery, people who cohabited formed societies to protect themselves, and their children from 'rogue' males.

The fact that the tree was reputed to have been a fruit tree stems from the fact that fruit is associated with female sexuality. A tree symbolizes the ability to express ideas in common language, and the ability to rise above the environment. It also symbolises that which connects heaven to earth, which is what the human spirit is about.

A person seeing that he or she is naked pertains to his or her becoming consciously sexually aware. Animals are not aware of their nakedness or of their sexuality. For that reason they do not feel embarrassed by, or sexually aroused by one another. Even when females are in oestrus, animals' sexuality is not driven by their desire for one another, but rather by an instinctive desire to copulate. An animal's sexuality is not its own. It is in service of the survival of its species.

To clothe himself symbolises a human making his or her sexuality his or her own.   No longer was it for a male to perceive a female's state of receptivity, and taking the liberty to approach her as if she were an animal.   No longer was it up to a male animal to first overpower other males, and then palm himself on a receptive female. Instead, it was for the woman to perceive her own need for sexuality, and to make her interest in a man of her choice clear.

In response to the Serpent's interference with the Creator's ambition to keep human sexuality tied to a cycle of receptivity, the Patriarch cursed the Serpent, and the woman. First, he rendered the Serpent less mobile, 'upon thy belly shalt thou go, and dust shalt thou eat all the days of thy life' (Genesis 3:14). [Wings are symbolic of a spirit collective's freedom to move anywhere without prior permission.]

Secondly, he declared a state of opposition between the woman and the Serpent, 'I will put enmity between thee and the woman, and between thy seed and her seed. [Seed here means 'spirit energy,' Genesis 3:15.] This enmity would result from the fact that the woman's seed would bruise the snake's head, while he would bruise her heel. What does this mean?

One person bruising another's head symbolises bruising that person in his will. What was the serpent's will? That the woman's sexuality should be her own. Why would she bruise the snake in his will that her sexuality should be her own?

In the garden, nobody worked, due to climatic conditions having favouring the availability of seasonal fruit. Adam was fruitarian like primates are, 'Of every tree of the garden thou mayest freely eat' (Genesis 2:16).

Following their exit from the garden, perpetual receptivity placed responsibility on the woman's shoulders. She could either have sex, or not. Pregnancy and the responsibility of feeding children, rendered her dependent on male favour, and male favour went to women who were willing to have sex, from which pregnancy again resulted.

Secondly, the woman lost her place in the Patriarchal collective, and accrued to the Matriarchal collective, which was a lower collective than the Patriarchal collective, a great loss in status from a spirit's point of view.

Following Adam's exit from the garden, the Patriarchal collective proceeded to reimpose animal sexuality on women by creating social rules that ensured women assumed a reticent sexual demeanour, in which men approached women in response to their need for sexuality, and not vice versa. This process was exacerbated by the imposition of Matriarchal values on people. The Matriarchal collective seeks to reduce spirits to souls, and then to reduce souls to alter egos, and alter egos to evil eyes. For this reason, Matriarchy sees sexuality to a tradeable commodity. This placed female sexuality in service of an emerging male need for domination, and ownership which remained part of Patriarchal societies, even after the age of Aries.

To further ensure female disadvantage, following Adam's 'fall from grace,' the woman was rendered impotent, 'thy desire shall be to thy husband, and he shall rule over thee' (Genesis 3:16). Now, this was one law given man at the beginning of time, and this time (the age of Aquarius) is the time of the fulfilment [ending] of the law.

Due to her incarnating from the Matriarchal collective, the woman would not receive a spirit, but only a soul. The spirit relates to work, while the soul supports a spirit. A soul thus looks to attach itself to a spirit, and support that spirit's quest for success.

To effect the outcomes her soul desired, the woman would thus look to the man in her life, who received a spirit. But his spirit had a mission of its own. By contrast to the physical woman, the physical man would live by the sweat of his brow, due to his receiving a spirit. Through the spirit, he would feel drawn to do a specific work. But he also received his own soul, who desired different things from his woman's soul. His interest in the woman was thus entirely sexually driven. Her life would thus be one of longing, until Apep could 'bruise her heel.'

To bruise someone's heel, is to destroy the karma that person came with [animal sexuality in this case.] While the woman bruising the snake's head thus pertained to women trying to relinquish control over their sexuality, the serpent by contrast, would strive to place the woman in control of her sexuality. This was 'the law' given Adam in Eden, and the ending of this 'law' was determined to be by 'the end of days,' that is, at the onset of the age of Aquarius. This would take five thousand years to effect, and came about during the last century when Apep [by this time the Incarnating spirit of the Eastern European collective], became the Incarnating spirit of the Northern European, and Eastern collectives, his having received new genes from outside.

For centuries women's need to fulfil their ambition through attachment to men, and men's indifference to women's ambition was mirrored in physical relationships of dissatisfaction between women and their men.

The beginning of the end of the law became possible when women began incarnating in 1955 with the same psychic arrangement as men, and when contraceptive hormones became available. This ended more than five thousand years of people living futile lives of domination over, and submission to, others. The age of Aquarius is about domination over self, and submission to the spirit's will to do its assigned work.

It is important to note that Genesis 3:16 represents a blatant statement of intention at literal intervention in man's genetic make-up, specifically to increase the human female's frequency of conception. It is indeed doubtful such a modification could have been brought about by any intervention, other than altering genetic arrangement.

Man's choice to own his sexuality, brought him the burden of his own physical support. It is important to note that, to work for a living did not amount to a 'law,' as the intention from the outset was to create a man who tilled the soil. The law here, pertained to the earth being cursed, and bringing forth thorns and thistles, 'Because thou hast hearkened unto the voice of thy wife, and hast eaten of the tree ... cursed is the ground for thy sake; in sorrow shalt thou eat of it all the days of thy life' (Genesis 3:17). This, man's work representing a struggle, was part of the 'law' that would end by the end of days, see 'Understanding Revelations.'

Adam's decision to eat from the tree of knowledge required their removal from the vicinity of the tree of life. Interestingly, when rules were stipulated about not eating these trees' fruits, the Creator significantly said nothing about not eating from the tree of life, in spite of later translators attempting to cover this apparent contradiction, 'But of the tree of knowledge, thou shalt not eat' (Genesis 2:17).

The reason why Adam would not have been ordered to abstain from the tree of life, is that Adam's eating from the tree of life would logically have depended on their having eaten from the tree of knowledge, first. Obviously, only then would they also have acquired the desire to want to achieve more in life years. Before Adam had thus eaten of the tree of knowledge, there would have been no danger of their eating of the tree of life, as they would have held no desire to be more than they were in any faculty whatever, least of all in years. The original instruction would thus logically have said nothing about not eating from the tree of life, as one evolutionary stage cannot be aspired to, before a previous stage had been attempted.

A living entity need reach an advanced stage of consciousness before it becomes capable of achieving growth while living continuously. Even today, humans tend to stagnate at certain stages of development, and then become rigid and resist further personal growth. Typically, they begin resisting new ideas, and new ways of perceiving matters. Some even resist accepting new thoughts that negate established values and perspectives, while most reject any notion of self development if it encompasses personal change.

As Adam did not eat from the tree of life, man's evolutionary upward spiral in consciousness remained tied to the evolutionary cycle of birth, and death, 'for dust [energy] thou art and unto dust shalt thou return' (Genesis 3:19), another law that would be fulfilled by 'the end of days.'

In spite of traditional religious interpretation, it emerges that Adam interpreted their new found status neither a curse, nor a fall. At the time of Adam's leaving the garden, the group of female individuals who had ventured beyond the boundaries of instinct were hailed 'Eve' [mother of all living.]

Moreover, to be a tiller of soil is liberating in the longer term, it could therefore not possibly have ever constituted punishment. Many people think that animals live careless, happy lives. However, even in tropical havens animals live miserable lives of struggle for bare physical survival. When we look at the great primates, we see their days occupied searching for roots, fruit, and herbs. When there is drought, or during seasonal change when food becomes scarce, they often go hungry, and many die.

That man moved from a lower to a higher state of evolution is supported by the statement that the Creator made clothes of skin for Adam and Eve to wear. Surely, clothing symbolically raises the mind above the body in importance. An animal's body determines outcomes for it. Our minds do. In addition, this paved the way for the most basic industry: transforming animal hide, and plant material into material for clothing.

Traditional ignorance had it that the Creator created man perfect, fully intending to give him eternal life on a platter, once he deemed man ready. However, that man had moved from a state of relatively lesser perfection to a state of greater perfection, and vice versa, is supported by verse 22 stating, 'Behold, the man is become as one of us, to know good and evil.' Knowing good from evil entails the ability to judge yourself independently from others' judgment of you, and to judge others independently of their actions. Evidently then, man's disobedience rendered him not less perfect, but indeed more perfect, and the story of Eden speaks then, not of man's fall, but indeed about the rise of man from animal consciousness to human consciousness.

BORN IN SIN

As a result of her subsequent dependency, the woman would survive due to her being at the receiving end of male favour. The man's favour would obviously be contingent on her serving his sexual purpose: a humiliating place for any energy entity to be. Here, the woman's sexual need of her husband became a secondary consideration, if not a non-issue. Sexuality centred around the wife retaining her husband's favour for the sake of physical survival.

111

This amounted to 'sinful' sexuality: a person doing one thing while thinking about another.

As everyone knows, children were often conceived in past years even when parents had no will to conceive children, but indeed resented child conception. Conceiving 'in sorrow,' was a woman conceiving children she did not want to conceive from a man she had no sexual desire for, but on whom she was ultimately physically dependent.

Being born in sin was to be born from a mother who thus conceived. In all this, nobody was doing their will, but instead fulfilling their desire for sex, and support, respectively. Outcomes in their lives came about as a result of sexuality they wanted with a person whom, for the most part, they did not want, but who supported their physical livelihood.

Like the woman, the man would not only be given to sinful sexuality, his work he would not do for the sake of his spirit's evolution, but mainly to support responsibilities he created for himself for lack of foresight. Doing one thing for the sake of another thing ultimately defines sinfulness.

Irresponsible sexuality however, not only resulted in sin, it also made it impossible for most people to deliver on their spirit's agreement with the universe. This amounted to cardinal sin [a term never understood by the church,] hence the ancient association between sex, and cardinal sin [failure to deliver on the life contract].

Instead of sexuality being a tool of self expression, and an expression of the power of self, as it will be in future years, it instead amounted to an exercise in energy imposition, and self denial, if not self sacrifice. As a result of traditional misunderstanding about the meaning of the sexual faculty, work and sexuality, which is meant to facilitate growth in consciousness, instead became tools of consciousness limitation, and power negation.

Even worse than having sex for support, or having sex with a person one does not want, is having sex for the sake of another. Here, one partner feels a morbid compulsion to sacrifice himself, or herself, to the upliftment of another. The worst kind of injustice a person can possibly inflict on his or her spirit it to have sex with a person whose spirit was incarnated from a lower spirit house than their own. [Spirits are very mindful of their relative status, expensively bought through many incarnations.] The conscious mind forcing the spirit to subject himself or herself to another's sexual advances against the spirit's inclination to leave the relationship, results in a spirit being rendered an alter ego, a massive drop in status for a spirit, and one too often experienced by many spirits today. Innocence [spiritual purity] is lost when a person does what he or she no longer wants to do. At the root of loss of innocence is the splitting of the emotional core from the physical experience as a result of corporal punishment during the early years, as the story of Ani indeed demonstrates.

CHAPTER 4

MAN'S EARLY EVOLUTION

If we choose to interpret biblical text as the church traditionally did, we have to concede that, at the point at which God reprimanded Cain, there were only three individuals on earth: Adam, Eve and Cain.

Were Cain one individual however, how could everyone who found him, slay him? Surely, one individual can only be slain once, while this verse refers to Cain being repeatedly slain. Add this to the fact that Genesis 5:2 clearly negates the interpretation that Adam was a male individual, and one is easily convinced that Cain was the name of a group or tribe of individuals, all of whom could be slain by everyone who found them.

115

According to the text, Cain was required to leave the Eden region following their extermination of Abel, and move to the land, Nod. I observed in Chapter 3 that the text made it seem that there were people around, and that some were genetically restructured, and placed in the garden, away from others not so restructured. This is supported by Cain's observation that everyone who found him [in Nod], would slay him. Surely, only if there were people outside Eden at the outset, could there have been people outside Eden, later. Moreover, only if people indeed existed outside Eden, could everyone outside Eden who found Cain, slay him.

The expression 'Adam knew his wife, Eve, and she conceived,' thus means that tribal sexual activity, following Abel's extermination, resulted in a tertiary tribe called 'Seth,' coming into existence some years after Abel's demise. In other words, several individuals were born following Abel's death, and they banded together under the leadership of an individual called Seth, one hundred and thirty years after the tribe Adam began proliferating outside the garden. To interpret the word 'son' as 'male offspring,' imposes an impossible meaning on the text. 'Son' may also mean 'product,' 'follower,' 'native' or 'subsidiary.'

A further possibility that emerges from the relation about Seth's separation from Adam, is that Adam and Eve were genetically different from one another. The text is written in such a way that it appears those products or 'sons' of Adam and Eve's reproductive efforts who were in Adam's likeness became known as 'Seth,' and lived separately *because* they were in Adam's likeness. In other words, they lived separately to escalate their 'Adam-likeness.'

Surely, the only reason why it would be stated that Seth was in Adam's likeness, would be because Cain and Abel were not. Had the types Adam and Eve been identical, or even simi lar in appearance, all their descendants would have been in their [Adam and Eve's] likeness, much as the products of our sexual reproduction are in our likeness.

This would also explain the eventual proliferation of culturally differentiated human tribes who had different ways of living, who eventually occupied different territories, and who eventually spoke different languages, 'These are the sons of Shem, after their families, after their tongues, in their lands, after their nations' (Genesis 10:31).

Following Seth's branching off as a sub-tribe, the tribe Adam continued proliferating for a further eight hundred years. The days of Adam therefore tell us about the number of years the first human kind or tribe proliferated before another tribe originated from it. It also tells us that, after Seth began proliferating as a separate tribe, Adam proliferated for a further 800 years before either disbanding, being assimilated into other tribes, or becoming extinct, 'And all the days that Adam lived were 930 years: and he died' (Genesis 5:5).

The first age of any man mentioned in Genesis 5 thus refers to the number of years a tribe of people existed before a new tribe stemmed from them. The second age given, is the number of years a tribe continued proliferating after the 'son' tribe it had given origin to, separated to form a new tribe. Typically, each tribe continued existing for a few centuries, before either disbanding, or becoming extinct. Towards the end of the age of Taurus, two hundred individuals from the tribe Enoch were taken to begin a new collective in Eastern Europe under the auspices of Apep, following Apep's leaving the Matriarchal collective due to his attempt to sexually empower women.

At around the same time, the Creator became aware that,

due to Patriarchal support, the Matriarch was again posing a threat to his intention to introduce Division, by the Matriarch creating social conditions not conducive to physical safety. The selective removal of atmosphere from areas occupied by the Matriarch, resulted in prolific rain in some places and freezing conditions in polar regions, already weighted as a result of the removal of atmosphere during the ages of Aquarius, and Leo. As a direct result, the ice shifted from the poles, causing upheaval to follow a significant flood. As the ice caps shifted, the earth's axis, already at 17°, tilted to 23°.

The evolutionary progression of man from Adam through Noah [the kind thought most suitable to continue human life following a catastrophic flood] brought about the shifting of the earth's axis, in turn brought about by the selected removal of atmosphere over areas occupied by Patriarchal, and Matriarchal collectives, is thus clearly outlined in Genesis 5, including the fact that, following a period of around one thousand years of proliferation, each kind 'died.' These 'ages of men' tell us a logical, interesting, and empowering story about man's early evolution.

While the significance of Genesis 5 is in the history of man's early evolution, and the reason for his creation, Genesis 4 defines the long misunderstood meaning of the concept of 'sin,' spoken about in the story of Cain [incarnated from the house of the Patriarch], who represented the second lowest spirit house, and Abel [incarnated from the house of the giants], who represented the highest spirit house.

The giants became vulnerable due to their sharing a geographical area with the Patriarchs, who incarnated from a lower spirit house, there having been five spirit houses at the time, the Matriarchal house having been the lowest.

The giants and their women preferred moving on their own, and living separately from others, and one another, each taking a keen interest in chemistry, patent medicine, astronomy, and astrology. Each had a vegetable garden, and some animals, and each one was completely physically independent.

People at the time knew the rules of the universe, and one rule states that, should a woman from a higher spirit house choose a man from a lower spirit house as a sexual partner of her own free will, her spirit house had the choice of either leaving her out at the end of her life, or accepting the man of her choice in with her. The first option is almost always taken by the spirit house, but this was either not known by the Patriarchs, or they simply hoped to be accepted. The Patriarchs at the time were less than half the giants' height, and far below them in consciousness, although not in arrogance.

Due to the giants' women refusing the Patriarchs as partners, the Patriarchs thought to eliminate the giants, thereby leaving their women with no choice but to have Patriarchs instead. They did this by incarcerating the giants' women. Giants who sought to free their women from Patriarchal incarceration, were singled out, and massacred by packs of Patriarchs. This went on, until it became apparent to the Creator that more than half the males had disappeared

Cain thus sought to use Abel's women to improve his own karmic standing, and Abel's defence of their women led to their demise, hence Cain's ejection from the Eden region.

The reason for the Creator's rejection of the Patriarch's offering, was that Cain sought to be whom Abel was, not by working, but by marrying Abel's women. Cain was thus not seeking to do well in his own right, using his own ability, but indeed to usurp Abel's karmic status by pushing into Abel's collective through marriage.

Cain and Abel were described in chapter 4 of Genesis in terms of their work. Their offerings represented the products of their labour, the result of their efforts. Abel's offering thus represented the labour of a man focussed on his task. Cain's offering was that of a man who sought to have what Abel had worked for, through marriage.

Sin is divided focus, or doing one thing with your mind on another thing. Cain was thus not looking at Abel's women because they wanted the women, but because they wanted to improve their karmic status through attaching themselves to the women, 'sin lieth at the door. And unto thee shall be his desire' (Genesis 4:7). It is each person's job to 'rule over him' (Genesis 4:7). The whole of life is about acquiring consciousness through effort.

Killing Abel, as if that could make him what Abel was, got the Patriarch banished from Eden, and cursed in the earth. To be cursed in the earth meant that Cain would never be able to grow their own produce, and would instead have to trade other products for food.

Following their chauvinistic extermination of Abel for anger about whom they [Cain] were, [the kind of anger that underlies crimes like rape], Cain became a builder of cities, or of a city, and city dwellers. As Cain had to trade other talents for food, his descendants became the 'fathers' of nomads, cattle farmers, metal smiths, and musicians (Genesis 20-2).

CHAPTER 5

FROM HERD RELATEDNESS
TO INDIVIDUAL DESTINY

It is important to draw a clear distinction between self sacrifice, which entails spending the individual lifetime serving others' purpose, thereby compromising self interests, and sacrifice for the sake of self, which is doing whatever is necessary, or giving up whatever need be given up, to do the work the spirit agreed to do, prior to its incarnating.

The story of Cain and Abel clarifies the importance of a person committing himself, or herself, to doing what is right for him, or her, and the folly of one person trying to get what another has, without effort.

The lives of Abraham, Sarah, Isaac, Rebecca, Jacob, Esau, and Jacob's twelve sons   demonstrate that, following the individual destiny is the source of personal power.

Secondly, their story illustrates that freedom from bonds of obligation, facilitates personal growth, 'Get thee out of thy country, and from thy kindred' (Genesis 12:1).

Thirdly, their respective stories leave one in no doubt that a relationship exists between personal conduct during life, and fate, following life. In other words, we do not only reap as we sow in life, more importantly, we proceed to reap after life, as we sowed in life. In fact, the saga of Abraham, Isaac and the ram (Genesis 22), exemplifies the extent to which Abraham understood that life was not about life.

But the parallel story of mankind's proliferation in a situation of growing scarcity, and climatic change, is one that depicts the human female's gradual fall from equality as Aries symbolism increasingly impacted human consciousness. As population density increased, man did not only lose the intimate connectedness with the Giver those early men enjoyed, women's social position simultaneously became increasingly compromised.

Understandably, population growth in a situation of scarcity would promote competition for scarce resources. In addition, the number of able soldiers at hand to defend tribal territory would virtually have determined tribal survival. For this reason, women's worth increasingly depended on their ability to bear male children. But female status was mainly eroded because the mother's contribution to a child's genetic make-up was not understood. Children were assumed to be the products of their fathers' seed alone. But female status was mainly eroded by the fact that women lost the right to marry when they wanted to, or to decide whether they wanted to, a right they had during the age of Taurus.

Jacob and Esau represented two different kinds of humans who incarnated from two different spirit collectives. Tradition has it that, when Esau and Jacob were born, Jacob took hold on Esau's heel, (Genesis 25:26). This obviously could not pertain to physical birthing dynamics. A new born infant's hand is first-ly too small to grab another infant's heel, and secondly, it lacks the coordination to do so.

To grab another by the heel is to accuse that person of hav-ing overstepped the boundaries of a karmic agreement.

Upon birth, the incarnating spirit connects to the body of the infant as it emerges from the womb. It hangs around the moth-er's body for some time before birth, especially when a specific birth time is required. The spirit without works with the infant within, and with the mother's spirit, pacing the birth to ensure the anticipated astronomy is correct. If birth is induced, or in cases of caesarian birth, the spirit needs permission to connect, as the astrology it came for is usually not met.

When twins are born, spirits often bicker as to which one will attach to the infant that emerges first. First born status is sym-bolically important to spirits, as the first born is usually more likely to become the head of his own spirit house, following life.

In the case of Jacob's and Esau's births the agreement from the start was that the spirit called 'Jacob' would attach to the infant born first, while the spirit called 'Esau' would attach to the infant born, second. When the first infant emerged however, the spirit who had agreed to wait for the second infant to emerge, instead attached to the first child, leaving the spirit who passively accepted his 'right' to attach to the first child, to wait for the second child to emerge. In this way, Jacob's first born right was taken from him.

Jacob grabbing Esau's heel pertained to Jacob's spirit symbolically accusing Esau's spirit of having contravened a prenatal karmic agreement, (Genesis 25:26).

The traditional interpretation that Esau sold his first born right to Jacob for a pot of lentil soup, is amazing indeed. If he did, why did Jacob not feel entitled to receiving Esau's blessing from Isaac? Why did he have to lie to get it? Moreover, why was Esau murderously angered about it, and why did he subsequently flee, as if he had done something wrong?

Jacob's twenty years with Laban was the price Jacob paid for usurping Esau's blessing. During his twenty years with Laban, Jacob was deceived, and treated unfairly. He paid twice the agreed price in life years for the wife he wanted. Through twenty years of incredible sacrifice for the sake of self, and focussed dedication to acquiring wealth, he lost his will to usurp others' rights, and instead focussed on earning his own place by his own effort. This resulted in his fortune eventually surpassing Laban's. As a result, he attracted Laban's sons' envy. When he eventually left to safeguard the possessions he had worked long and hard to acquire, he accepted that his wives and children belonged to Laban, as was the contract when the husband of a woman was a serf to her father. He was however, determined not to lose what he had fairly earned, (Genesis 31:4-16).

Upon his return to his own people, he finally parted with his cunning and cowardice, (Genesis 32). As a sign of his peaceful intent, Jacob sent his brother a gift. He no longer cared about his lost first born right. He did not feel justified about usurping Esau's blessing, he did not get an army of his own together, he did not blame his mother. Instead, he separated his wives and children from his party of servants, and remained to face Esau alone.

His willingness to pay for past wrongs with his life if need be, introduced the final shift towards his becoming the head of his spirit collective by the time of his death. This came about as a result of Jacob's wrestling with a 'man' [spirit], while awaiting Esau's arrival.

Any injury sustained by the spirit is felt at the physical level, as if it occurred at the physical level. However, medical examination will reveal no damage to the physique. If the injury is permanent, as a hip dislocation would be, the pain would be permanent, and the walk uneven in spite of there being no physical hip dislocation. As reward for his not having gone down to this opposing spirit, his name became 'Israel,' the name of the Incarnating spirit of the Hebrews during the age of Aries.

The whole story about Jacob and Esau was a story about two spirits doing as best they could to ensure the supremacy of the respective spirit collectives they became the Incarnating spirits of, following their lives. Their story reveals that we reap as we sow in life, but more importantly, that our personal conduct during life produces results for us, following life.

That life is not about life, that life is about growing the spirit in consciousness, and that each person connects with a spirit house to which he or she returns following life, is most clearly spoken about in the 'blessings' Jacob pronounced over his sons before his death. The meaning of Jacob's blessings of his sons becomes clearer when juxtaposed to blessings some noteworthy individuals received in the story of Abraham.

Some blessings pertained to material rewards for commended behaviour during life, such as land (Genesis 12:7), many descendants (Genesis 16:10), personal wealth (Genesis 27:39), and so on. However, when we look at those individuals who were most favoured, it is possible to see that, over and above the material rewards their blessings encompassed, their blessings also contained elements that did not relate either to their lives, or to the lives of their descendants, and I shall focus on those blessings.

Abraham's blessing (Genesis 22:17) went, 'thy seed shall possess the gate of his enemies.' Now, this blessing cannot be interpreted against the facts of Jewish history. There is firstly little historical evidence of Jews ever possessing their enemies' gates, much the contrary. Secondly, the Israelites did not genetically descend from Abraham. Here, the word 'seed' means 'spirit energy,' those born from Abraham's spirit house, not his physical descendants.

Moving now to Isaac's blessing of Jacob, and Esau, Isaac told Jacob that he would be lord over his brethren, and that his mother's sons would bow down to him. Now, Esau never bowed down to his brother, much the contrary, '[Jacob] bowed himself to the ground seven times, until he came near to his brother' (Genesis 33:3). Moreover, Esau never served his brother but 'went into the country from the face of his brother, For their riches were more than that they might dwell together' (Genesis 36:6-7).

Clearly here, not Jacob, nor his physical descendants, but those born from Jacob's house would tend to assume leadership positions over other men born from the same spirit collective. Similarly, those born from Esau's house would live by their swords, and serve their brothers [others born from the same collective,] (Genesis 27:28-40).

To unravel the meaning of these blessings that, upon closer scrutiny, bore little relevance to either the lives of the people who received them, or their descendants', we need look at Genesis 49, which tells the story about Jacob calling his sons together to reveal to each one what would befall him 'in the last days.'

Before continuing, it is important to understand what is meant by 'last days.' Genesis 49:10 is commonly understood to be a prophecy about the coming of the Messiah, 'The sceptre shall not depart from Judah, nor a lawgiver from between his feet, until Shiloh come; and unto him shall the gathering of the people be.'

It is important to know that an Incarnating fraternity's time on a planet amounts to twelve ages. The Creator arrived on earth with the Patriarch, and the giants to incarnate under the paradigms of Patriarchy, and Division, at the beginning of the previous age of Aquarius. Great ages are deemed to begin at the start of ages of Aquarius, and thus the shift from one great age to another, is known as 'the end of days,' and that is the time in which we now find ourselves, see 'Understanding Revelations.'

Jacob thus referred to a status that would come into effect plus minus four thousand years from the time of his uttering the blessings, that is, around the time of the shift from Pisces to Aquarius. From this perspective, it would not be unreasonable if one asked how a state of affairs that would eventuate that far into the future could possibly have been of interest to any of his sons? For example, the 'blessing' given Reuben, 'thou shalt not excel' (Genesis 49:4) would have no bearing on Reuben's life, as the prophecy pertained to what Reuben would be by 'the end of days,' that is, at the time of the sceptre departing from the house of Judah, that is, those who, by that time, represented mosaic law.

[It is interesting to note that, although Reuben was the only one of Jacob's sons who felt any compassion for Joseph, or any sense of responsibility for Jacob's feelings regarding Joseph, we see that Reuben is yet another example of a person who became the victim of a parent's intent to disadvantage his child, much as Esau was. Instead of confronting Reuben about having sex with his concubine, and telling him he will have no more of it, or ceding the concubine to Reuben, Jacob instead kept silent and harbored a grudge against his son.]

Be that as it might, to answer the question about Jacob's prophecy, and what bearing it would have on Reuben and the rest of his sons, we need look at what happens to people, following life. 'And the Lord spake unto Moses, and be gathered unto thy people; as Aaron thy brother, was gathered unto his people' (Deuteronomy 32:48-50). Clearly, people, following their lives, are reunited with a spirit collective to which they belonged, before. Equally importantly, physical relatedness does not necessarily link to spiritual relatedness.

The question arises as to whether the prophecies that these people received, which did not relate to their fates during their physical lives, or to the lives of their descendants, instead pertained to what happened to them after they were 'gathered unto their people?'

To better understand what may have followed their physical existence upon their return to their respective spirit houses, we need turn to Exodus 1. Biblical histology has it that the Pharaoh ordered two midwives to kill each Jewish boy at birth. The two midwives thought that such action would be wrong, and risked their lives refraining from following the Pharaoh's order. This constitutes doing the will of self.

It is said that, in response to their righteousness, 'it came to pass, that he [God] made them [the midwives] houses' (Exodus 1:21). Here one is looking at two spirits doing their work, and doing their will, against instructions, at risk of life and limb. The actions of the midwives were thus the actions of 'men' [spirits], and not women [souls]. A spirit is a 'man,' and a man does his will. God thus did not build them material houses to live in, but made them 'houses,' that is, spirit houses which are energy entities that incarnate spirits.

The women referred to in Exodus 1 were thus judged righteous enough that, following their lives, they were made spirit houses to whom specific evolutionary growth paths were assigned. These they could realize by incarnating people under specific astrological variables, and during specific time periods during the age during which they were allowed to incarnate.

This means that the spirit collective expands itself by way of raising individuals who exceed what may be expected of them [given their abilities and circumstances], to the status of new spirit 'houses.' Since the spirit collective proliferates itself by promoting deserving individuals to the status of new spirit houses, from the collective's perspective, a person is only profitable when he or she exceeds their duty and expands the number of houses in the collective, as a result.

Reuben and the rest of Jacob's sons thus became new spirit houses following their lives, and the blessing he bestowed on each son, constituted the evolutionary growth path each spirit that son would incarnate would grow through following. Only from this perspective do Jacob's prophecies begin to make sense, and are we able to understand how Jacob, Esau, and Jacob's twelve sons were affected by the respective blessings they received during their lives.

Each person grows in consciousness, and energy density by struggling to overcome the obstacles in their path to personal success. For example, the evolutionary growth path of those incarnated by Reuben's house would run through personal struggle against psychological barriers to success. On the other hand, those who belonged to the house of Zebulun would be drawn to living marine related lives, while those incarnated by the houses of Simeon and Levi would fall prey to cruelty. This is obviously not to say that, if someone belonged to a 'house,' that his or her fate was sealed. Instead, it means that they grew through expressing themselves in certain ways, or by living in certain ways, or by overcoming certain obstacles.

But Jacob's prophecy regarding what karmic fates the houses of Simeon and Levi would represent in particular, makes it clear that his 'blessings' referred to something infinitely more profound than an old man simply wishing his sons the best, or worst of luck upon his death. Their blessing, 'Simeon and Levi are brethren; instruments of cruelty are in their habitations' (Genesis 49:5) relates to individuals who are born into circumstances where they fall prey to bullying, and victimization.

In fact, the words 'I will divide them in Jacob and scatter them in Israel' (Gen. 49:7), sound like common madness when applied to the actual physical lives of Simeon and Levi, or even their descendants. Yet, it makes perfect sense when we understand that Jacob's words pertained to a distribution of victims over all other evolutionary growth paths.

Interestingly, poverty was nobody's fate. Both Jacob and Esau received the fatness of the earth. However, dependency often results from a combination of arrested consciousness, and genetic factors, which combine to create a personal reality of scarcity, as everyone knows. In particular, individual intolerance to postponing short term rewards in favour of longer term gain, is a hallmark of people who are unable to create wealth.

Israel was thus the collective name of Jacob's spirit house, which incorporated the twelve houses of his sons, hence Jacob's authority to determine the fate of his sons, following their lives.

THE AGE OF AQUARIUS

At the beginning of each new age, a new blue print is given man that guides the direction of evolution of human consciousness. That direction is determined by the symbolic meaning assigned the incoming age.

By the end of the age of Taurus, a 'great herd' consciousness had come into existence, as is evident from reading the story about the feeling of collective belonging that existed in people around the time of their planning to build Babel, 'let us make us a name, lest we be scattered abroad' (Genesis 11:4). Here, people lived in extended groups, and women conceived children whose fathers they did not even know. Children were routinely sold into slavery and prostitution as early as age five, although it was not uncommon for two year old's to have been taken by slave traders who paid twice the price for infants. By the age of twelve such children were discarded without any means of self support, their having worked as sex slaves in the so-called 'temples' without payment, and only in exchange for food.

The age of Aries brought a blueprint that forced a small herd lifestyle during which only concubines' children were sold into slavery. This trend continued until the beginning of the age of Pisces, when people became monogamous, resulting in this practice comparatively slowing down. During the age of Pisces, the Arabian people mainly were slave traders who mainly bought slaves from tribal chiefs in Africa.

As the age of Pisces began receding during the 1950's and 1960's, a cultural revolution inaugurated a new social paradigm which fundamentally changed Western consciousness to produce Western societies of personal freedom, and a degree of equality of the sexes that never existed before in all man's history.

Pisces represents the ending of relationships, while Aquarius demands uncompromising allegiance to the cause of self. The age of Pisces represented the beginning of the 'fulfilment [ending] of the law,' [given Adam in Eden.]

At the beginning of each new age, a great spirit emerges as the Incarnating spirit for the incoming age. This spirit entity sets up the collectives so that the evolutionary ideals he or she envisages, can be realized. At the same time, the 'face,' or appearance of the Incarnating spirit assumes a form that symbolises the paradigm of the age.

During the age of Pisces, the Incarnating spirit assumed the face of a donkey to symbolise the self sacrificial tendencies of that astronomical sign, hence Jesus' entry into Jerusalem on the back of a donkey. During the age of Aries, it assumed the face of a ram, figure 45.

The symbol for Aquarius is the double-headed eagle. The eagle is associated with territoriality, vision, and power-parenting. The twin head symbolises the twin spirit whose addition to the human psyche after the age of forty five represents the process of so-called 'rebirth,' which will result in man's becoming a 'fraternal' spirit, and inaugurate his entry to a new level of consciousness.

Above all, however, the eagle symbolises the emerging 'spirit mate' relationship within, which will be reflected in the spirit mate relationship without. This will involve brain evolution that has already begun in about 4,500 individuals. This brain evolution will result in an additional brain area which will free the right hemisphere from left hemisphere domination. [The right hemisphere usually receives inhibiting signals from the left hemisphere.] This change will enable two spirits to be given to each person who dedicates his or her life to achieving their highest potential, while seeking their highest enjoyment of life.

Here, sexuality serves the purpose of each partner's understanding his or her karmic contract, and the role each is to play in bringing about the outcome each one incarnated to bring about in their own life. The sexual attraction is such that the spirit rises to reveal its innate life work to the conscious mind. [The danger here is getting involved in a permanent relationship before the spirit mate enters the life equation, usually after age forty. Obviously, alternative sexual relationships should be enjoyed until the spirit mate arrives.]

For the first time in man's history, man is ready to begin learning about the spirit, its place in the universe, its relationship to the conscious mind, and how life revolves around growth in consciousness through self realization. During this time, the human spirit will begin incarnating at a higher level of consciousness than it did during the age of Pisces, which represented a higher level of consciousness than the age of Aries.

Depicted on the cover image are two spirits at the fifth level of consciousness, entering the Hall of Judgment during Egyptian times. The whole of life is about growing the spirit in consciousness, tenacity, and understanding of the law of cause and effect.

Fig 1 Apep, the collective of the alter ego during the age of Taurus, was widely considered the Archenemy of the Patriarch, and opponent of the Creator. Apep lost his wings (symbolic of the ability of the collective to move anywhere it wanted without permission), following his interfering with human sexual programming during the time of Adam's evolution in the garden of Eden during the most recent age of Taurus.

Fig. 2 When atmosphere, or spirit energy is withdrawn, refraction is lost, and the sun's light appears dim, as if something has shifted between the planet and the sun when in fact, what was between the planet and the sun had been removed. The air becomes 'thin,' no rain falls, and no crops can be grown above ground. Walking above the surface becomes a frightening, lonely, and threatening experience.

Fig 3 Nut (the great spirit which is the atmosphere), symbolically giving birth to the sun. 'Sun' here means 'light due to refraction.' The increased light intensity enables an Incarnating fraternity to evolve life on a planet.

Fig 4 The bovine, in the process of being imbued with the self sacrificial tendencies associated with the sign of Taurus, at the beginning of one or the other age of Taurus.

Fig 5 Beb is the chief symbol of Matriarchy. When the Matriarch was ousted from Africa, and the middle East, they settled in South America, moving several structures from Heliopolis to that continent. They incarnated in South America, Tibet, America, and Africa.

Fig. 6 The Matriarch since the age of Taurus, symbolised by the dog, the proverbial 'keeper of contracts.' The Matriarch arrived on the earth plane with slaves they claimed they wanted to evolve to a higher level of consciousness on a planet where water was available. The Matriarchs were banned from the earth plane one hundred and fifty years ago.

Fig 7 Osiris sitting in his shrine. A shrine is a space occupied by
the energy of a great spirit. Behind Osiris are his twin soul, Isis,
and Nephthys. The green pillar-like structures circled above are
energy 'screens' the Incarnating spirit erected around his place of
work to keep out interfering energy.

Fig 8 The human spirit begins to assume the form
of the body at the age of thirteen/fourteen. The
spirit enters the body for the first time at age nine.
Before that, the spirit is loosely attached to the
back of the spine.

Fig 9 Ani leaving his tomb (the white light house type structure in the background). Behind him, his house of spirits hovers, waiting to lead him towarrds the collective, while his spirit house, (symbolised by the small tree before the tomb), awaits the outcome of Ani's judgment.

Fig 10 Ani and his wife Thuthu, entering the Hall of
Judgment. During ages of Patriarchy, and Benign
Intervention, the wife awaited her husband's arrival
at the entrance to the collective as they were judged
together. The ankh in Thuthu's right hand indicated
her status as alter ego in their relationship.

Fig 11 The spirit house is symbolised by the small tree above. Within it, the cosmic mother presides over the lives of individuals she incarnated. The cosmic mother is in service of the Sprit Collective to which her spirit house belongs, and incarnates under the guidance of the Incarnating spirit. The spirit house incarnates as many spirits as it has guardian angels to oversee.

Fig 12 A spirit collective appears as an energy cloud, or energy ribbon. The collective 'character' is expressed as an archetype of sorts. Depending on the energy quality of the collective, it either moves dynamically from place to place, or settles in one place for a time before moving on. It listens for spirits calling for collection, then moves to gather them.

Fig 13 A terra cotta face (symbolic of the soul) was weighed against a feather (symbolic of the spirit). This weighing measured the soul's level of evolution against the spirit's. Inside the square above the soul, Ani's house of spirits looked on, see figure 14.

Fig 14 Ani's house of spirits was given by the house of Osiris. In other worrds, Ani was incarnated by the house of Osiris.

Fig 15 The Devourer of the Unjust, sitting behind Thoth, who was jotting down Ani's karma.

Fig 16 The alter ego was symbolised by a tongue. The energy of the tongue was channelled into the foot of a female baboon. The behaviour of the baboon in the presence of alter ego energy was observed. The baboon's behaviour gave a measure of the alter ego's evil, or inclination to embarrass the spirit, and put others' interests above those of the spirit.

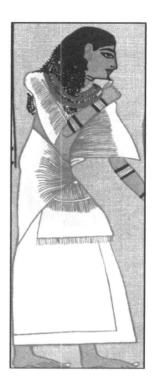

Fig 17 Following Ani's and Thuthu's judgment, Thuthu, having been judged as if she were Ani's soul, channelled her energy to Ani. Ani's having become proverbially 'one flesh' with Thuthu, is reflected in the change in Ani's spirit's appearancey The dark areas indicate areas where the spirit attaches itself to the body..

Fig 18 Ani and Horus, approaching Osiris' shrine. Horus wore the head dress of the house of the Patriarch. The house of the Patriarch was mainly symbolised by the falcon head.

Fig 19 A single layer of spirit energy behind Isis and Nephthys, suspended from Osiris' lower self. Compared to Thuthu's spirit (fig 8), which consists of a number of layers of spirit energy, the single layer of energy appears distinctly diffuse, and not at all expensive in appearance. This demonstrates the difference energy density makes to physical appearance.

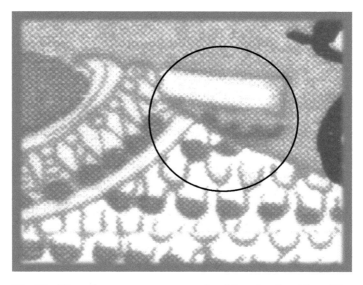

Fig 20 The alter ego peers over the falcon's shoulder. The alter ego relates to the evil eye, a collective of male spirits who seek to impose their will on others.

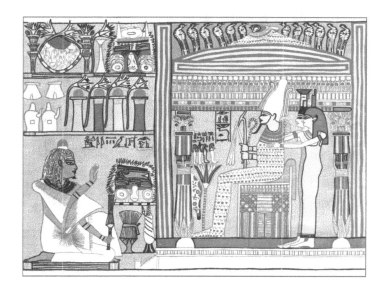

Fig 21 Ani sitting before Osiris.

Fig 22 A single leaf of spirit energy ready programmed to incarnate as an evil eye from the house of the Patriarch suspended from the Patriarch's lower self behind Osiris.

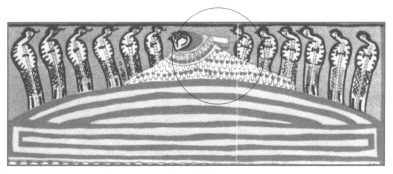

Fig 23 Twelve serpents (each relating to a house of astrology) are positioned on either side of the house of the Patriarch, each pronouncing an oracle over the falcon (symbol of the Patriarch). Behind the falcon's head, the alter ego can be seen leafing layers of energy over the falcon's body. Each energy leaf contains the 'evil eye,' or psychic message asociataed with the house of the Patriarch. Figure 19 shows how Thuthu's spirit leafs are imbued with karma by Osiris. Part of this karma relates to the evil eyes lying over the house of the Patriarch entering the spirit leafs through Osiris' feet. The ready-programmed spirit leaf is shown in figure 22. Once a spirit leaf who received an evil eye is imposed on a human's body at birth, it acts exactly as the evil eye portrayed behind the house of the Patriarch. The alter ego contaminated spirit showers evil eyes over the house of spirits, so that each person who associates with a person incarnated by an 'evil eye' collective, runs the risk of receiving an energy leaf containing an evil eye (psychic message) from the person whose spirit was thus contaminated. Enlarged below are the evil eyes covering the falcon.. Each evil eye looks down a nose.

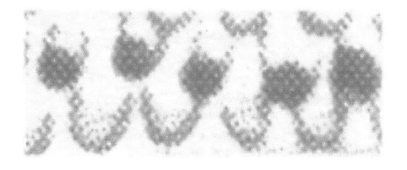

Fig 24 In his hand, Ani holds a small bundle that appears as a sheath of wheat. Beneath the stack, is a larger sheath. These sheaths made of energy are transparent 'tubes' which attach the spirit to the body. Within each tube, memory of life events is digitally inscribed. At the time of judgment this energy was released over the low ampere rod shown above the larger bundle of sheaths. As the energy passed from the sheaths over the rod, a symbolic image of events that transpired during the person's lifetime, appeared as an energy image ('stack') above the rod for all to see. In this case, a duck with its wings broken off, may be seen.

Fig 25 Circled beneath the stack, is a low voltage lamp through which Thuthu's energy flowed towards Osiris' shrine. The colour of the lamp revealed the frequency, and amplitude (and thus the level of consciousness) of the energy moving through it.

Fig 26 A female person of high birth, almost certainly his wife, broke Ani's spirit. The figure on the left indicates a woman who commanded slaves, usually a woman of high birth. The symbol in the woman's left hand, represents an instrument of cruelty, as indicated by the two prongs which suggest splitting the soul from the spirit. A broken spirit does not do its own will, instead, it does the will of the alter ego overlay which shifts inbetween his soul and spirit.

Fig 27 The circled figure indicates psychic overlay, or energy overlay, from a man. Under Matriarchal law, men were not allowed to impregnate their wives without the wife's persmission.

Men who did, were whipped on their buttocks by the Matriarch himself. As a result of emotional upheaval during the process, Ani's sexuality was overlaid by a man with contraceptive ideas in mind. As a direct result of Ani's consent to subject himself to this punishment, the Patriarch declared his spirit an alter eog.

Fig 28 The bird of prey symbolised a person who used another without giving anything in return. The presence of this symbol meant that Ani allowed himself to be sacrificed to another's purpose.

Fig 29 Further spirit overlays attached Ani to Thuthu in such a way that he never thought about leaving the relationship. Under primitive conditions, people's lives were simplistic, and child rearing was almost the only avenue of personal growth. Failing to reproduce virtually amounted to failing in the life calling.

Fig 30 Due to Ani's adherence to Thuthu's Matriarchal persuasion, both Ani and Thuthu were under the Matriarch's auspices by the end of their lives. This condition is symbolised by the eye above the two figures below. The figure on the left of the circle represents Ani, whose higher mind had been overlaid by the Matriarch, and the figure towards the right represents Thuthu, incarnated from the house of Nephthys, the Incarnating spirit of the house of the Matriarch at the time.

Fig 31 The large bundle of energy sheaths beneath the small stack before Ani constitute the psychic hair, or the proverbial 'hair on your head' which is counted. This energy connects the higher mind to the higher self, or house of spirits.

Fig 32 Ani's higher mind (circled above his head), contained karma given him by the Incarnating spirit to draw the same kind of experience to him that befell him in previous lifetimes. This karma was symbolically represented by the contents of the large stack above Ani's head, enlarged below.

Fig 33 Circled above is karma Ani received, following his first lifetime during which his higher mind received energy overlays from others. These overlays transferred energy from Ani's brain to the collectives to which the overlaying individuals belonged.

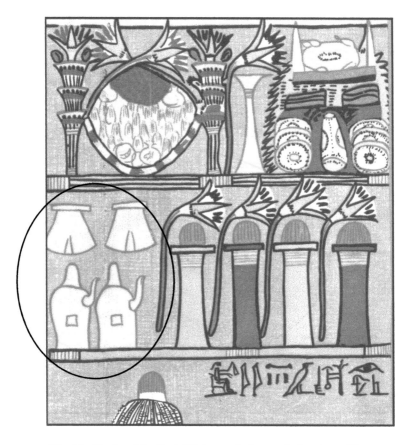

Fig 34 During his first lifetime, Ani married twice. The urns with detached lids indicate that, in each case, the marriage was not consummated.

Fig 35 During his second lifetime, Ani fell prey to a mother who was an evil eye. An evil eye is a person whose eyes continually deliver a psychic message to those the authoritarian mind considers below him, or her in the human order. The figure to the left, indicated by the arrow, indicates that, almost typical of those who fall prey to authoritarianism, Ani identified with the paradigm his mother represented, and sought, in turn, to impose what his mother had imposed on him, on others. This means that, through his long term association with a person who was an evil eye, Ani himself became an evil eye.

Fig 36 Osiris' higher mind (the area indicataed by his white helmet), in contact with the Patriarch's lower self (circled). The lower self is the soul's 'brain,' where minor karma is stored in what is known as minor serpents.

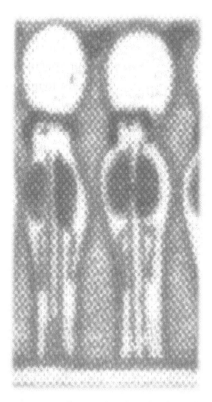

Fig 37 Above the head of each minor serpent found in the lower self, a tiny crystal ball is balanced. Each crystal ball contains a drama symbolising a life event that profoundly effected outcomes in a past lifetime. Whenever life change brings about circumstance similar to circumstance that transpired in a past life, the drama contained within the relevant crystal ball is activated, and keeps playing, until karma is balanced.

Fig 38 The deities on the lotus in front of Osiris relate to the fist four houses of astrology.

The energy given by the deities before Osiris settle as serpents in the higher self. Each serpent pronounce oracles pertaining to astrological outcomes to the house of spirits. Connection to the higher self is given the deserving individual by his Incarnating Man (spirit).

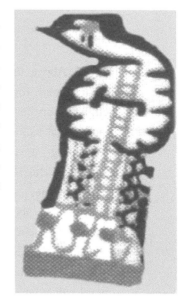

Fig 39 The Patriarch's spirit was given by the house of Horus, symbolised by the falcon head.

Fig 40 The spirit house is symbolised by a tree in which the cosmic mother resides. The spirit house keeps all the surplus spirit leafs a spirit accumulates during its lifetimes. When the spirit has completed a growth cycle at any given level of consciousness, it is able to move to the next, higher level of consciousness, provided it has enough energy in store to give it the energy density required to enter a higher level of consciousness.

Fig 41 A spirit is released from so-called 'curses' at the end of a lifetime. Curses were primarily symbolised by small rodends and snakes, which were deemed to differ from serpents. The serpent was associated with the spirit's healing, while snakes were associated with energy forces that undermined the spirit. During ages of Division curses are not given.

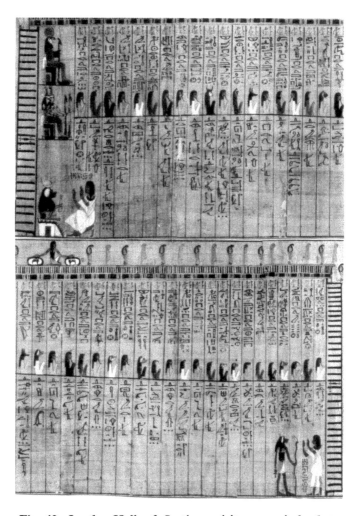

Fig 42 In the Hall of Justice spirits were judged to determine the extent to which they possessed negative survival traits. Each survival trait was symbolised by a so-called 'spirit animal.'

Fig 43 The Eden Story was misunderstood by the church, due to early interpreters' alignment with Matriarchal values. The Serpent represented a spirit collective. This collective either channelled a man it had incarnated, influencing him to speak to the women who were standing below the tree, or it directly channelled a woman standing below the tree, giving her ideas about her sexuality, and how to conduct herself in such a way that her sexuality would become her own.

Fig 44 Following the human female's choosing conscious sexuality over animal sexuality, the Patriarchs gave the Matriarch control over the female collectives. Here, the Patriarch is in the process of dividing the bull (symbolic of the age of Taurus), in the presence of the Matriarch during the most recent age of Taurus. The Matriarch's inclination to sacrifice is immediately apparent in the symbolism surrounding the ritual. Compare the symbolism to the majesty implied in the same ritual portrayed in figure 4.

Fig 45 At the beginning of each age, the 'face' of the Incarnating spirit changes to symbolise the paradigm of the age. In the foreground, the Incarnating spirit of Aries is in the process of imbuing man with the properties associated with Aries, while Thoth (behind) adjusted his life span accordingly.

Sa   Hu   Hathor   Hor

ephthys, and before him, upon a lotus stand the

us   Isis & Nephthys   Nut   Seb

Osiris Throned within a shrine. Behind him are Isis
children of Horus.

Ani justified kneeling before Osiris

Tefnut   Shu   Temu   Ra-Harmachis

Anubis testing the tongue of the Balance

Thoth recording the result of the weighing.

The Devourer of the

Unjustified

Horus introducing Ani into the presenc

enet and Meskhenet, the
esses of birth.

Ani's soul, Ani's Embryo, Ani's Luck of
Destiny

Ani and his wife Thuthu entering the Hall of Judgment

Re
Go

of Osiris

SELECTED BIBLIOGRAPHY

1   The Ancient Egyptian Pyramid Texts (R.O. Faulkner), Aris & Phillips, Warminster, England.

2   The Egyptian Heaven & Hell (E.A. Wallis Budge) Open Court, Chicago and La Salle, Illinois.

3   The Egyptian Book of the Dead, The Papyrus of Ani (E.A. Wallis Budge) Dover Publications, Inc., New York.

4   The Ancient Egyptian Coffin Texts Vol. I Spells 1-354 (R.O. Faulkner), Aris & Phillips Ltd., Warminster, England.

5   The Ancient Egyptian Coffin Texts Vol. II Spells 355-787 (R.O. Faulkner), Aris & Phillips Ltd., Warminster, England.

6   The Ancient Egyptian Coffin Texts Vol. III Spells 788-1185 & Index (R.O. Faulkner), Aris & Phillips Ltd., Warminster, England.

7   The Ancient Egyptian Book of the Dead (R.O. Faulkner), Universeity of Texas Press, Austin.   Published in Cooperation with British Museum Press.

8   The Gods of the Egyptians, Studies in Eguptian Mythology with 229 Illustrations, Including 6 in Full Colour, Vol. 2, (E.A. Wallis Budge).

9   Reading Egyptian Art, A Hieroglyphic Guide to Ancient Egyptian Painting and Sculpture (Richard H. Wilkinson), Thames & Hudson.

10   An Egyptian Hieroglypnic Dictionary (E.A. Wallis Budge), Vol. I, Dover Publications, Inc., New York.

11   An Egyptian Hieroglyphic Dictionary (E.A. Wallis Budge), Vol. II, Dover Publications, Inc., New York.

12   *The Mystical Qabalah* (Dion Fortune), The Society of Inner Light, 38 Steeles Road, London.

13   *Experiencing the Kabbalah,* (Chic Cicero, Sandra Tabatha Cicero), Llewellyn Publications, St. Paul, Minnesota, USA.

14   *Holy Bible (Translated out of the original tongues and with the former translations diligently compared and revised by his Majesty's special Command)*, Cambridge University Press.

15   The Chumash (Stone Edition), Mesorah Publications, New York.